Country Classics
25 Early American Projects

Country Classics
25 Early American Projects

Gloria Saberin

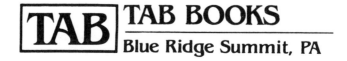

TAB BOOKS
Blue Ridge Summit, PA

Every effort has been made to assure the accuracy of the instructions in this book, but no warranty is given nor are results guaranteed. The author and the publisher have no control over the conditions in which the information is applied and consequently disclaim any responsibility for the results obtained.

FIRST EDITION
FIRST PRINTING

© 1991 by **TAB BOOKS**.
TAB BOOKS is a division of McGraw-Hill, Inc.

Library of Congress Cataloging-in-Publication Data

Saberin, Gloria.
    Country classics : 25 early American projects / by Gloria Saberin.
       p.   cm.
    Includes index.
    ISBN 0-8306-7587-6 (h)   ISBN 0-8306-3587-4 (p)
    1. Woodwork. I. Title.
  TT180.S324   1990
  684'.08—dc20   90-49720
                              CIP

TAB BOOKS offers software for sale. For information and a catalog, please contact TAB Software Department, Blue Ridge Summit, PA 17294-0850.

Questions regarding the content of this book should be addressed to:

Reader Inquiry Branch
TAB BOOKS
Blue Ridge Summit, PA 17294-0850

Acquisitions Editor: Kimberly Tabor
Book Editor: Susan L. Rockwell
Production: Katherine Brown
Cover Photography: Fruit basket photo bottom right corner, courtesy Sterling Photography, Camp Hill, PA. All other cover photos, courtesy Paul C. Saberin, Farm Out Graphics, Saint Thomas, PA.

Contents

Acknowledgments

I am thankful to the special people whose help made this book possible. I am especially grateful to Frances Carnahan and *Early American Life* magazine for the permission to reprint the projects that they first inspired and then published. For the beautiful color photographs, I thank Sterling Commercial Photography and Farm-Out Graphics. For solving my woodworking problems throughout the years, I thank my neighbors and fine woodworkers Nieca Witter, Mark Heckman, and Harry Davis. My husband and partner, Paul Saberin, has drawn the plans and projects and has given me years of encouragement while I researched and made these reproductions. Thanks also to Sallie Pfoutz and Bonnie Brechbill for their advice and typing.

Many years ago, an old sea captain taught me to carve, chisel, and sand a piece of mahogany until it became a fish, thus sparking an interest in working with wood that has enriched my life. I wish I could thank him, too.

Preface

I researched and made the reproductions featured in this book because I wanted to duplicate those charming and functional survivors of our country's early years. Since I possessed more patience and curiosity than tools or knowledge, researching, drawing plans, finding appropriate wood and crafting each piece took an incredibly long time. Each project was a new and challenging puzzle, but even when I made a miscut or split a section of wood after hours of work, it was all worthwhile.

The best way to learn woodworking is to choose a simple plan and start working. Tools and wood will teach you something new each time you work with them. Begin with a few good, basic hand tools and softwood, and make a dancing man, woodchoppers, or a spoon rack. Add more tools as you need them and gradually try more complex projects.

I hope the patterns in this book will coax you along and that you will enjoy the pursuit of woodworking in the tradition of our American forefathers. Making the kind of items that the early settlers made will bring much of our history to life.

One fact that is important to keep in mind is that when I write of early craftsmen and woodworkers, they were usually not professional craftsmen. The men who made the original pieces that I copied were probably farmers and householders who had built their own homes and also fashioned whatever furniture and accessories were needed. They might have brought a trunk, chair, or even a bed to their new homes, but everything else was made on-site by family members and their neighbors. As settlements grew, real cabinetmakers made the more complex furniture but the simple pieces and toys were still made at home. In rural and mountain areas of our country, this homemade tradition is found even today.

If you want to learn more about early craftsmen, their tools and methods, read the wonderful books by scholarly artists such as Eric Sloan and Roy Underhill. These works are fascinating as well as informative. If you want to learn about using modern tools, consult *The Woodworker's Illustrated Benchtop Reference* by William Spence and Duane Griffiths, TAB Book No. 3177. It will answer all your questions about tools and how to use them.

Introduction

Do hard-to-find Early American household furniture, accessories, and toys catch your eye at antique shops and auctions? Several years ago, treasures from our past could be purchased for a few dollars each. Today, such objects command a price that only museums, devoted collectors, and dealers can afford. However, if you like to work with wood, here is a relatively inexpensive way to have interesting, useful country pieces. By following the plans in this book, you can make authentic reproductions of wooden objects common to eighteenth- and nineteenth-century country homes.

I selected the reproductions featured in this book for their unique charm and simplicity. I chose both utilitarian and decorative furniture, accessories and toys to make an Early American country collection that can be crafted by novice and experienced woodworker alike. These plans were derived following my careful research of antiques in private as well as museum collections. Some of the projects were initiated by magazine assignments but others were the result of my desire to reproduce some special items seen in my travels. I use the reproductions in my eighteenth-century log farmhouse: the knife tray holds silverware, the softwood wall box decorates my family room, the basket carrier holds quarts of produce each summer, and the dancing man delights children at family gatherings.

The simple, clean lines and functional designs of these pieces are as useful and appealing today as they were two hundred years ago. Make them yourself, decorate and finish them to complement your own home, and then display them proudly alongside your real antiques.

Notes for
the Woodworker

The projects in this book are reproductions of furniture, accessories, and toys that were made from native woods by early settlers using homemade tools. It is possible to make all of them with hand tools and basic woodworking experience, but do not hesitate to use a band saw, scroll saw, drill press, router, or lathe if you have the skill to use them. Early craftsmen used the best tools available to them, and we should too.

Even if you use power tools, you can achieve the desirable authentic antique look by keeping a hands-on approach to each project. Hand-finish your work, doing the sanding and scraping by hand. Use wooden plugs to cover countersunk screws, and avoid obvious shortcuts such as using dovetailing attachments. It is far better to change the plans and eliminate dovetails completely than to make factory-style, evenly spaced ones. The irregularity inherent in the use of hand tools gives a more genuine look to the finished reproduction.

Some of the photographs in this book show the original antiques in their present setting. Other photos are of my reproductions, none of which are artificially aged or antiqued in any way. When you finish your own work, you might want to distress or antique it to fit in with your authentic antiques.

THE PATTERNS AND HOW TO ENLARGE THEM

Throughout this book I have provided plans for curving areas wherever possible. I have gridded the curving sections in order for you to enlarge them more precisely. In these cases, I have indicated the size to which the grid squares must be enlarged before transferring to the wood stock. The method I use is to lay out a grid of desired size on a large sheet of paper. Number and grid the coordinates on both the small grid in the book and the larger grid. Then, transfer the coordinate points to the large grid. Next, using a French curve, connect the points. Check the configuration several times as you proceed.

An easy way to enlarge plans is to use an enlarging copier at a commercial printer or copy center. Copy the pattern at book size. Then enlarge the pattern until the grid squares are the required size for a full-sized pattern. I like this method, for after I have the pattern at full size, I can make several copies to use later. For very large pieces, you might have to cut and paste several sheets of the enlarged copy together.

A pattern can be transferred to the wood with the use of carbon paper. Instead of using carbon paper, I often rub a soft pencil on the back of the pattern and then trace as in Fig. 1. Another method is to cut a template of cardboard from the pattern and trace around it to transfer the design to the wood stock. This works well when you need to fit several pieces on the board around knot-holes and other imperfections. One of my octogenarian friends, Harry Davis, always glues the paper pattern directly to the wood and cuts through paper and wood at the same time. This solution is perfect for the intricate patterns he cuts.

Fig. 1. Author tracing pattern onto wood

WOOD

The pleasure of working with wood increases as you do more and more of it. A well-sanded or turned piece is as satisfying to the hand as it is to the eye. When a beautiful section of wood is crafted into an appropriate project, it is a joy to make and a pleasure to use.

It is not necessary to use fine wood for everything you make. As you work with different kinds of wood, you will learn how they can be used to best advantage. The first step in making a project is to determine which qualities of wood

Table 1. Working Characteristics
of Woods Commonly Used by American Settlers.

Wood	Strength	Weight	Other Properties
Ash	strong	heavy	Bends well, holds shape after bending
Basswood	weak	light	Easy to carve with knife or hand tools; fine grain, light, even color.
Birch	strong	heavy	Hard to work, but good for turning; fine grain
Cherry	strong	medium	Medium to work, good for turning, handles furniture, beautiful, often reddish color.
Hickory	strong	medium	Easy to work when green; good for chairs, etc. Good for splitting when green.
Maple	strong	medium to heavy	Difficult to work by hand, but often beautiful and excellent for furniture.
Pine	soft to medium	medium	Relatively easy to work, good for nailing. Varies according to type of pine; some are good for carving, but weak; others are stronger and good for simple furniture, toys, etc. Can have large, loose knotholes in some boards. Light color.
Poplar	medium	light to medium	Easy to work, fine texture, yellow to greenish color.
Walnut	strong	heavy	Medium to work, rich color, even grain. Good for turning and nailing. Excellent for small pieces and furniture.

are necessary to its successful construction. Ask yourself: Does the project require wood with strength, fine grain, beauty, and color? Should it be easy to carve and/or turn? (See Table 1).

How you intend to finish the project also influences the selection of wood. A painted piece does not require the beautiful wood that a stained piece does. If you choose your wood carefully according to the item you are making, the tools you have, and your ability, your woodworking will give you successful results and much pleasure.

When purchasing lumber for your project, allow enough for squaring off the ends and for making a few mistakes on cutting out patterns or for avoiding knotholes or other imperfections.

Most of the materials lists give the exact measurements for the finished piece of wood. When a one-inch board is indicated, it means an actual full inch by measure after being dressed or surfaced on both sides. Some of the thicknesses required might be difficult to find in ordinary lumberyards. Wood today is usually cut thinner than was the custom in colonial times. If you cannot locate the thickness of wood specified, you might have to order it custom-cut and planed.

When a project requires a very large piece of wood for a part such as a table top, join together several pieces of the desired stock by gluing and blind-doweling edge to edge. If you are doing this yourself, you will need large furniture clamps such as pipe clamps and a method of making the edges perfectly straight before joining. Alternate the direction of the end curve in adjacent pieces in order to lessen the chance of the board twisting and curving out of shape after you join it into one large section.

Occasionally, building supply houses sell wood already joined into large sheets for shelving, table tops, or counters. Take advantage of these oversized boards when you can.

When I go to lumberyards, supply houses, or auctions, I carry a metal measuring tape and a list of wood that I will need for future projects. Farm auctions are a good place to find old, full-cut lumber and table tops. Be careful when cutting such old boards to avoid buried nails and parts of hinges that could damage your saw blade.

When you purchase your wood, pick it out yourself. Check carefully for straightness and freedom from large blemishes such as loose knotholes and roughness. After you complete a few projects, you will develop a feel for the kind of wood that will make up easily. Trust your eyes and your hands as they feel the wood's surface. If you can locate a salesman who is himself a craftsman, he can be a great help in steering you to suitable wood.

Look through bins of leftovers from custom milling orders. Often I find just the pieces I need for a small project in some discard pile, thus saving the trouble of special-ordering a small amount of a certain size. If you do have to order lumber custom-cut or planed, purchase enough for several projects at once. This will save both time and money because with set-up costs a large order costs only a little more than a small one.

Very thin boards, such as those needed for the dancing man toy, the knife tray, and Noah's ark, can be found at hobby or craft stores. They are well finished on all sides and perfect for light work.

TOOLS

The projects in this book can be made without a wood shop or complicated power tools. Many small items such as the dancing man, the spoon rack, and the woodchoppers are easy to fashion with a coping saw, an X-Acto knife set, and a hand drill.

Sometimes I make a small project or parts of a larger one while sitting outside or working on a tray by the fireside. The animals for the ark, for instance, are fun to carve at craft fairs or festivals. People often tell me they would like to make things of wood but feel they need a complete workshop before they can start. All you really need is space, good ventilation, and a sturdy bench or table in order to begin.

If you are just getting started at woodworking, buy some of the basic tools and add others when needed. I suggest starting with hand tools and an electric drill. My initial tool kit included the following:

- crosscut saw (10 teeth to the inch)
- coping saw
- keyhole saw
- 16-ounce claw hammer
- tack hammer
- wooden mallet
- pliers, regular and needle nose
- set of screwdrivers, regular and Phillips
- set of chisels
- brace and bits
- eggbeater drill
- rasps and files, straight and curved
- nail set
- doweling centers
- marking gauge
- awl
- jack plane
- metal measuring tape
- carpenters square
- plumb line
- level
- metal bench rule
- utility knife
- X-Acto knife set and blades
- clamps
- woodworking vise

Buy the best tools possible and keep them sharp and the handles tight.

Over the years I have added some simple power tools and now have a table saw, a band saw, a scroll saw, a drill press, a router, and two belt sanders.

I have my power tools mounted on portable work tables so I am able to move them around in the shop and even outside when the weather permits. It is fun to work outdoors, especially when sanding or cutting large amounts of wood. I enjoy woodworking in the fresh air, and I hope you will try it. If you move power tools outside, be certain you have heavy-duty extension cords, and arrange them so you will not trip over them.

Power tools require less strength on your part and make the work go much faster. Add these when you feel you really need them. If you would use a power tool only occasionally, it might be more prudent to borrow it or to have another craftsman make that special section for you. When I need turning done, I often take the wood to a local woodworker who is an expert at the lathe. Since it is difficult to find beautiful, large wood suitable for turning, it is sensible to have it cut by a master turner instead of taking the chance of ruining the piece by turning it myself.

When you purchase power tools, do not use them until you know how to do so correctly and safely. Be certain they are mounted securely on their stands and have safe electrical hookups.

Power tools are a helpful option in woodworking. If you are planning to make several of one item, they are almost essential, unless, like former president Jimmy Carter, you prefer the actual manual crafting of each piece. He follows the pioneer spirit closely, felling the trees and proceeding with fashioning his hickory chairs in the exact methods used by his Georgia forebears.

The use of power tools does not detract from the appearance of reproductions as long as the finishing is done by hand. I prefer to do dovetailing and mortising by hand as I like the work, and the irregularity of the handwork adds to the charm of the completed piece. Adapt these patterns to suit yourself. Whether you wish to follow the early craftsmen in actual methods of production or to use the most modern tools available, you will enjoy the projects in this book. All were first made long ago by men taking pride in their creativity.

SAFETY

Safety is an important consideration when working with any kind of sharp implement, and especially when woodworking. With a few precautions, you can make woodworking as safe as any daily household task. Here are basic guidelines for your workshop.

1. Keep your floor clear of all debris.
2. Keep your floor dry to prevent shocks or slipping.
3. Don't wear loose, floppy clothing that can catch in your tools.
4. Keep your hair pulled back securely if it is long.
5. Wear safety glasses or a face shield.
6. Keep your tools sharp and the handles tight.

7. Unplug all power tools when not working with them or when changing blades or servicing them in any way.
8. Don't use a power tool unless you know how to use it properly.
9. If you have to use an extension cord, use a heavy-duty cord with three prongs.

FINISHING

After you complete the assembly of a project, you will be ready to proceed with the finishing. The entire finishing process often takes longer than the construction, and it is equally important to the success of your work. A good, well-applied finish protects the wood from dirt, moisture, heat, and small abrasions, as well as enhances the appearance of the reproduction.

Some of my instructions include suggestions as to the finish suitable for the project. However, it is not my intention to instruct in finishing methods or to limit your choices. As long as you use a technique and product appropriate to the style and period of your reproduction, it will appear authentic. After you decide how you want your finished piece to look, consult an authoritative source and follow the instructions exactly. There are dozens of wood-finishing products available today and many good books on the finishing techniques used in colonial America.

If the wood you have crafted is particularly beautiful or if you wish to have it match other unpainted furniture in your home, you could choose a wax, stain, or varnish-finishing coat. It would be sad to paint over walnut or birdseye maple, whereas a plain pine or basswood would be enhanced by a painted decoration. Be aware of the wood and its character as you plan the project. If you know you want a painted piece before constructing the project, choose your wood accordingly.

Painting techniques used during the colonial period of our country include sponge painting, marbling, stencilling, wood graining, and folk designs. The colors that were commonly used were mustard yellow, grey-green, grey- or teal-blue, and barn red. The Pennsylvania Dutch added very brightly colored designs to their furniture. Milk paints similar to the very early ones are available again today and would be suitable for almost all of the projects in this book.

Whichever finishing method you select, proper surface preparation is essential. It includes sealing the wood, filling small defects, sanding, and staining if desired. This is perhaps the dullest part of the entire construction process, but it is vital if the finish is to enhance the completed piece.

After repairing any defects in the wood, start sanding. Wipe with a clean cloth between uses of progressively finer grits of sandpaper. If you want a weathered or rustic look to your reproduction, you might want to round the edges and distress the wood to simulate wear. I do round the edges, but my personal preference is not to distress the surface. On fine-grained wood, I like to use wire wool for my final sanding. On some woods you will want to apply a wood sealer, but if you do, check the label because the sealer must be chemically compatible with the coat used over it.

If you stain wood to add color or heighten the grain, be sure to wear light-weight plastic gloves to protect your hands. Stain is almost impossible to remove from around the fingernails.

I like to apply stains with a rag and wipe off immediately with another cloth. Use a lint-free rag, as you don't want lint stuck to the surface of your piece. Repeat the staining until you have the desired effect, and then let it dry overnight before proceeding with a top coat.

In all the surface preparation and applying of paints or varnishes, use high-quality brushes and rags. It is important to avoid brush marks, hairs, and lint, which might mar your finish. I find it necessary to do the finishing in an area removed from any woodworking. Either move your project out of the area or refrain from sanding or cutting for a couple of days before painting or varnishing a piece.

The freedom to individualize a project by choice of finish is one of the rewards of making it yourself. I have made many knife trays, and finished each differently according to where it was to be used. Even though the piece is a reproduction, you can make it truly your creation by the choice of finish.

SUGGESTED PROCEDURES

1. Study the drawings and read all accompanying text.
2. Make a complete list of materials needed including all small items such as glue, nails, screws, plugs, hinges, sandpaper, etc. My materials lists do not always include all these small fasteners.
3. Determine which tools are necessary in order to construct the project.
4. Buy everything you will need to complete the entire project.
5. Enlarge the pattern to working size and cut any templates required.
6. If there are any complicated procedures such as dovetails or mortises, cut a practice set on a scrap of the same wood you are using for the project. Be sure the grain is aligned in the same direction as on the pattern. When you are confident that you can do the procedures correctly, continue to step 8.
7. If you decide to use an Easy-To-Do version, make adjustments to the pattern at this time.
8. Transfer the pattern to the wood using a sharp pencil, a knife, or a scribe.
9. Cut out all parts and sand well.
10. Make a trial assembly to make certain all parts fit together squarely and tightly.
11. Take apart and reassemble with glue and fasteners as needed.
12. You might want to stain or distress the wood at this time. If you want a slightly aged look, sand the edges at this time.
13. After the glue is completely dry, smooth again with very fine sandpaper or steel wool.
14. Wipe down with a lint-free cloth slightly dampened with turpentine before starting the finishing process you have selected.

PART 1

Small Household Accessories

Whether living in a substantial city home in the well-established settlements of Massachusetts, Pennsylvania, or Virginia or in a log or sod house at our western frontier, the early American housewife made her house into a real home with small useful and decorative accessories. The practice of individualizing a home with items possessing appealing design or special memories is just as important to today's homemakers. In this time of multi-unit identical townhouses and standardized store-bought furniture, it is remarkable how similar rooms can be made entirely different by the addition of well-chosen details.

I have selected the small projects in this section for their special charm and their reflection of times past as well as for their continuing usefulness. The love and care that was crafted into the originals is evident in the design of the knife tray, the spoon rack, and the wall box. Simpler versions of these antiques are often seen, but these particular antiques exhibit such attention to detail that they are truly special.

I like to believe that these pieces could have been handcrafted by a husband as a special gift for a young bride living far from relatives in a sparsely furnished frontier home. That these items have survived to the present proves that they were indeed treasured household accessories. They were used until badly worn, but they were not discarded with other, less-cherished pieces.

Travel in the early periods of our country's settlement was slow and hazardous. Imagine the pioneer families moving into unknown regions and carrying all their possessions with them by wagon, horseback, or small boat. A little-known fact is that thousands of settlers actually pushed and pulled all their goods in hand carts for hundreds of miles through forests, plains, and mountain ranges in their search for a place to establish a home. It is easy to understand why very few furnishings were carried with them. The small treasured items that they did take were all they had to remind them of home and old friends.

Make your reproductions of these treasured antiques with care and feeling, and you will have created a family heirloom of your own.

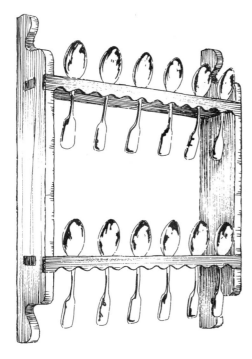

Fig. 1-1. Spoon rack.

Spoon Rack

Racks for spoons, plates, pipes, and other items were in common use in early colonial times. Taverns, inns, and private homes used racks to keep everyday articles readily available as well as to display items of beauty and value. Spoon racks often held pewter, nickel, or silver handmade spoons (Figs. 1-1, 1-2).

The original of this spoon rack was handcarved of softwoods (Fig. 1-3). It had much use, as shown by its softly rounded and worn edges. Most of the scallops on the trim were worn down so far that I nearly mistook the trim for a ragged straight piece with odd notches in it rather than the finely handcarved, curving section that it was originally. (Fig. 1-4) At present the original piece is nailed together with finishing nails, but I suspect that when it was constructed it was only fine-fitted and glued. When the early glue disintegrated, it was nailed together rather than reglued.

This copy of an eighteenth-century spoon rack is easy to make and can be used to hold a collection of early spoons or as a display shelf for other small treasures.

Choose your wood and finish to suit your own home and collection. Softwoods with a dull antique finish are best if you plan to hang it in an Early American style ''keeping room'' to display either pewter or soft silver spoons as the original was used. In a more formal room, walnut or cherry wood with a rubbed oil finish will fit in nicely. Paint with a colonial paint and stencil a Pennsylvania Dutch design on the sides and trim to achieve a more ''country'' look.

Fig. 1-2. Reproduction spoon rack.

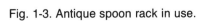

Fig. 1-3. Antique spoon rack in use.

Fig. 1-4. Worn trim on antique rack.

MATERIALS

- Fine-grained wood
- 2 pieces, $1/2 \times 2^1/2 \times 17$ inches for sides
- 2 pieces, $1/2 \times 2^5/16 \times 13$ inches for shelves
- 2 pieces, $3/16 \times 3/4 \times 13$ inches for trim
- 2 small brass hangers, $1/2$-inch wide or less to fasten on back top of sides for hanging up rack
- Carpenter's glue
- Finishing materials as needed (I used sandpaper, wire wool, and antique dull finish varnish).

CONSTRUCTION TIPS

Use a knife to carve trim. I used an X-Acto knife with a #11 blade. The joints should fit snugly. Cut the end pieces first, trim, and sand. Then cut out the shelves roughly. Fine fit to joints in sides. Do the same with the trim. After all fits well, stain if necessary. Assemble and glue in place. Finish as desired. Add hangers using tiny screws (Figs. 1-5, 1-6, 1-7).

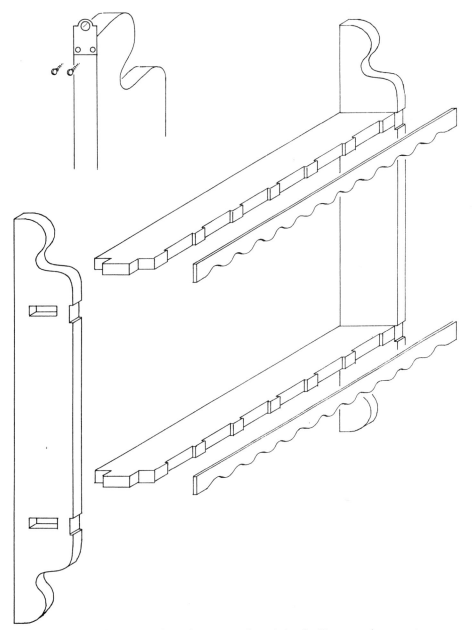

Fig. 1-5. Exploded view of spoon rack and detail of hanger placement.

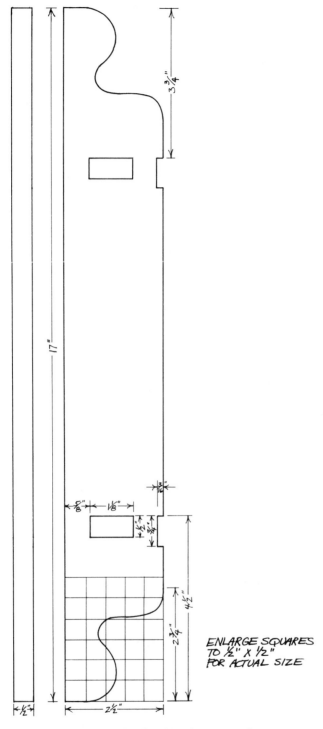

Fig. 1-6. Plan for side of spoon rack.

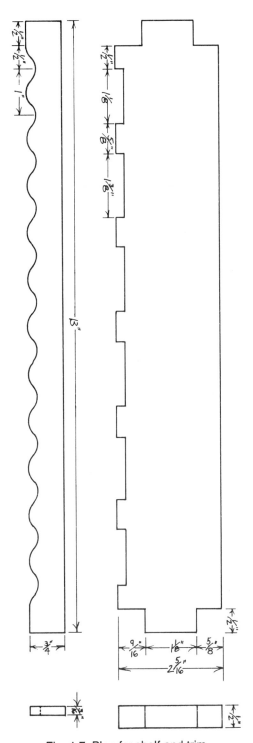

Fig. 1-7. Plan for shelf and trim.

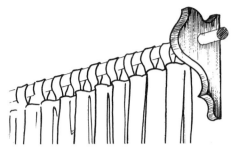

Fig. 2-1. Curtain brackets holding rod for tab curtains.

Brackets for Tab Curtains

The homespun that curtained the earliest American windows was tacked to the window frame or hung against it with a cord running through a narrow, hemmed tape at the top. Cloth was valuable; tabs attached to the tape extended the length of the curtain somewhat and helped to extend its life. Today's tab curtains, an important decorating element in American country rooms, still aren't much more complicated. Rather than a string and nails; however, wooden brackets supporting a dowel are a tidier way to hang them (Figs. 2-1, 2-2).

All you need is a wooden dowel heavy enough to support the weight of the curtains without bending and long enough to suit the window to be covered. The brackets that hold the dowel can be in several classic shapes; choose the one that best suits the size of your window and the room. Any sturdy, easily cut wood can be used; choose wood that matches your woodwork, or paint or stain it to match. Cut the pattern so the grain of the wood parallels the wall. I used inch-thick wood for the brackets; it finished out at about 3/4-inch thick. If necessary, adjust the dowel hole to fit the size of the dowel you are using. Rods longer than four feet should be at least an inch in diameter.

Mount brackets on the side of the window frame, on the outer edge of the frame, or on the wall beyond it.

MATERIALS

- Wood—pine, maple, or walnut, one-inch thick
- Sandpaper
- Stain
- Varnish or paint

CONSTRUCTION TIPS

Countersink screws, and cover the hole with plastic wood or a small wooden plug. To accommodate a wooden plug, drill first for the screw and then redrill the same hole to a depth of about 1/4 inch with a drill bit that is the diameter of the plug you want to use. Finish as desired, mount the brackets, sand over the fill plug, and touch it up to match (Figs. 2-3 through 2-6).

Fig. 2-2. Curtain brackets in use.

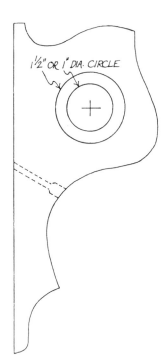

1/2" OR 1" DIA. CIRCLE

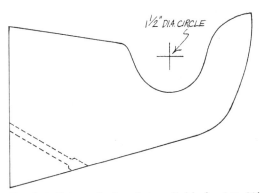

1/2" DIA. CIRCLE

Fig. 2-4. Pattern for brackets suitable for 1-to 1¼-inch rod.

Fig. 2-3. Pattern for brackets to hold ⅞-to 1¼-inch rod.

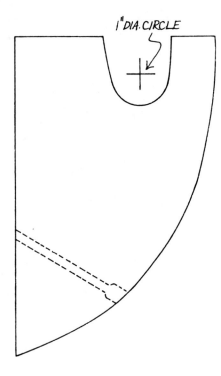

1" DIA. CIRCLE

Fig. 2-5. Pattern for brackets suitable
for 3/4-to 1-inch rod.

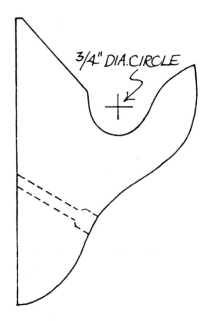

3/4" DIA. CIRCLE

Fig. 2-6. Pattern for brackets suitable
for 1/2-to 3/4-inch rod.

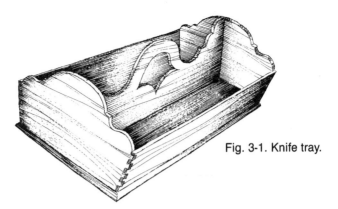

Fig. 3-1. Knife tray.

Knife Tray

Knife trays were very popular household accessories in Colonial America. Designed to hold tableware, they were made in various sizes and of many different woods. The old rural trays are often pine, poplar, and maple, but fine ones such as those used in the Massachusetts or Virginia colonies are more sophisticated and made of mahogany, cherry, or walnut that has been polished to a shine as lustrous as the silverware it holds. Almost every colonial restoration in America has several knife trays on display.

Since trays of this type were so common in early American households, they are still relatively easy to find at auctions and antique dealers. Don't expect the low prices of a few years ago, however, as they are becoming sought after for today's country homes.

The tray that I copied for this project was made in the 1700s. It has a beautiful curving design on the center panel and the end panels. I have used this pattern with several woods, some which I stained to show off the dovetailing and some which I painted, such as the one I use in my kitchen. The pattern is fun to construct and would make a cherished gift for a dear friend (Figs. 3-1, 3-2).

Start with an easy-to-carve and dovetail wood such as basswood or pine. If you are timid about the dovetailing, practice on some scrap wood, and then tackle the project.

Fig. 3-2. Reproduction of 18th century knife tray.

MATERIALS

Preferred wood: Fine-grained pine, basswood, cherry, or maple.:

- 1 piece, $1/4 \times 5 \times 13$ inches for center panel
- 2 pieces, $1/4 \times 4^{9/16} \times 8$ inches for end panels.
- 2 pieces, $1/4 \times 2^{11/16} \times 13^{1/4}$ inches for side panels.
- 1 piece, $3/8 \times 8 \times 15$ inches for base.
- Sandpaper, small brads, carpenter's glue, stain or paint, varnish

CONSTRUCTION TIPS

Cut the center panel from $1/4 =$ inch stock, sand, and set aside. Cut base rectangle 8×14 inches from $3/8$-inch stock. Round upper edges as on plan, sand, and set aside. Stain, if desired, at this time. Cut two end panels from $1/4$-inch stock. Rough cut without dovetails, which are done later. Rout out $1/4 =$ inch wide and $1/6$-inch deep channel on each panel, as on plan. Using a coping saw and chisel, cut dovetails on each side of the end panels. Cut two sides of $1/4$-inch stock. Rough cut; do not cut dovetails at this time. Bevel upper and lower edges $1/16$ inch. Taking one corner at a time, mark each side on the end grain, using the dovetails on end panels as your pattern. Cut out carefully, leaving extra wood on each tail so it can be individually sanded down to fit those on the end panels. When all the dovetails fit together neatly, assemble the entire top section without glue. Insert the center panel in channel on the end panel and make any necessary adjustments. When all fits well, take it apart and stain if desired. Reassemble, gluing the center panel in channel, and gluing dovetails if necessary. Using small brad nails, nail through the end panels into the center panel where needed to secure. Do not use more than two nails on each side. Center the completed top section on the base. Glue in place, and nail from the bottom up to secure. (two or three nails per section). Varnish, if stained, or paint (Figs. 3-3 through 3-7).

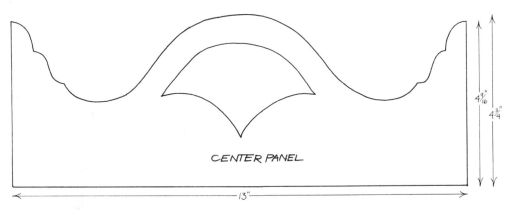

CENTER PANEL

$4^{9/16}$"
$4^{3/4}$"

13"

Fig. 3-3. Plan for center panel of knife tray.

 END PANEL TOP VIEW

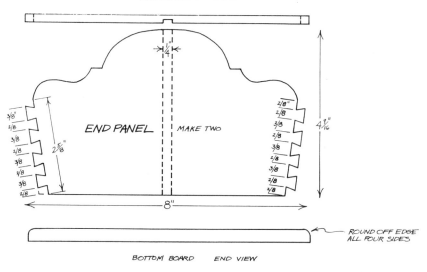

END PANEL   MAKE TWO

1/4"

2/8"
2/8
3/8
2/8
3/8
2/8
3/8
2/8
2/8

3/8"
2/8
3/8
2/8
3/8
2/8
3/8
2/8

2⅝"

4 9/16"

8"

ROUND OFF EDGE
ALL FOUR SIDES

BOTTOM BOARD   END VIEW

Fig. 3-4. Plan for end panel of knife tray and cross section of bottom board.

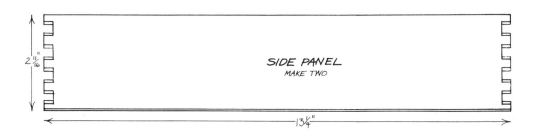

SIDE PANEL
MAKE TWO

2 11/16"

13¼"

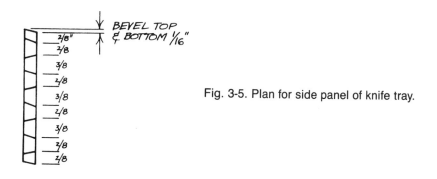

BEVEL TOP
& BOTTOM 1/16"

2/8"
2/8
3/8
2/8
3/8
2/8
3/8
2/8
2/8

Fig. 3-5. Plan for side panel of knife tray.

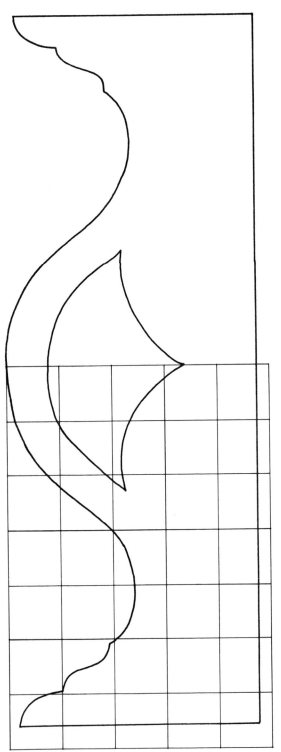

Fig. 3-6. Gridded pattern for center panel.

If you decide not to do the dovetailing but want a knife tray, follow these directions (Fig. 3-8). Cut the side panels a full 13¼ inches long, omitting dovetailing pattern. Cut the end panels ½ inch shorter by eliminating the dovetail sections on each side of end panel. Assemble as other directions, but nail through sides into end panels with tiny finishing nails. Don't forget to glue before nailing together.

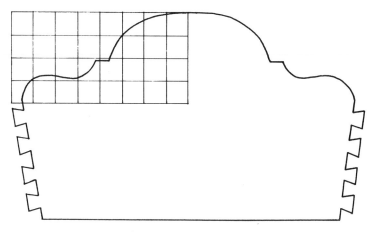

Fig. 3-7. Gridded pattern for end panel.

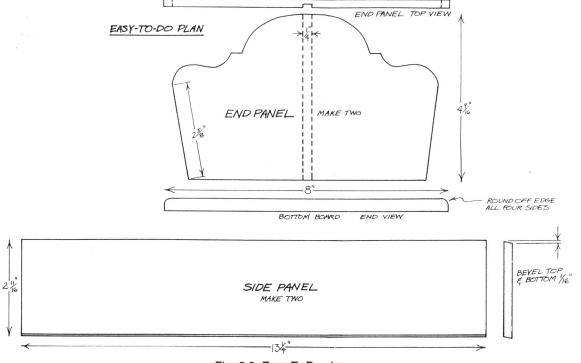

Fig. 3-8. Easy-To-Do plan.

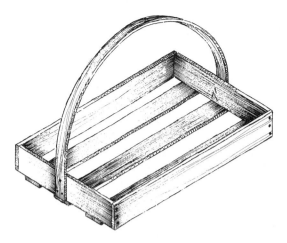

Fig. 4-1. Basket carrier.

Basket Carrier

Basket carriers like this one have been used for many years, various types can be found at auctions and antique shops in rural areas. They are perfect for picking a variety of fruits and vegetables for a meal. Mine is made to hold six quart-size wooden containers, but you can adapt the plan to hold any number and size of boxes that you prefer (Fig. 4-1).

This pattern for a basket carrier is copied directly from one that I own, which is over one hundred years old (see Fig. 4-2). I still use it daily in the summer to collect berries and other garden produce. In the fall, it holds apples and acorn squash. It is also perfect for carrying craft projects and small tools from place to place.

Fig. 4-2. Antique basket carrier.

Basket carriers are actually baskets in themselves but are called *carriers* for they usually hold an even number of small berry baskets. The traditional handle is bentwood, and if you have never bent wood before, this is a good project to try (Figs. 4-3, 4-4, 4-5). If you prefer an easier version, there is a straight-handle pattern to use as an alternative (Figs. 4-6, 4-7).

My original basket carrier is rough finished and plain, but I have made several with berries and vines painted or stenciled on the sides (Figs. 4-8, 4-9). I also like to varnish my carrier as I often put it on the ground when using it.

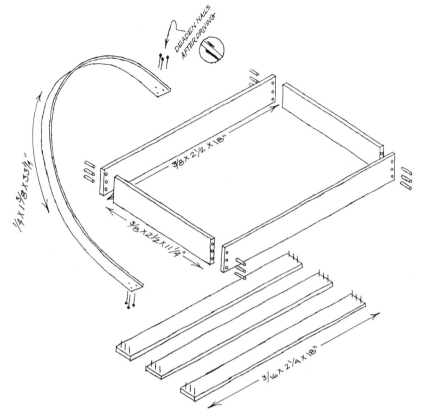

DEADEN NAILS AFTER DRIVING

1/4 X 1 3/8 X 33 3/4"

3/8 X 2 1/2 X 18"

3/8 X 2 1/2 X 11 1/4"

3/16 X 2 1/4 X 18"

Fig. 4-3. Exploded plan for basket carrier.

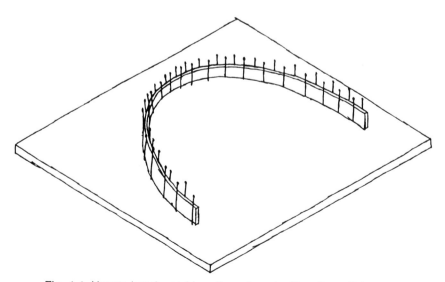

Fig. 4-4. How to bend wood handle on board with nails outlining curve.

Fig. 4-5. Deadened nails on original basket.

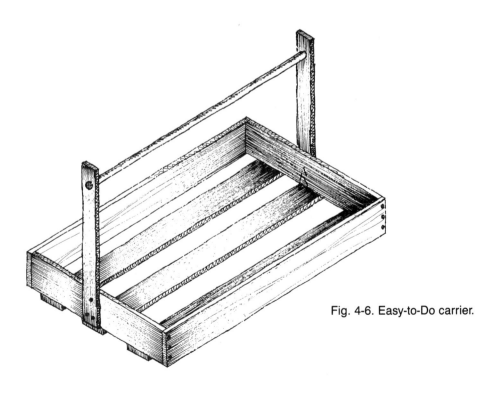

Fig. 4-6. Easy-to-Do carrier.

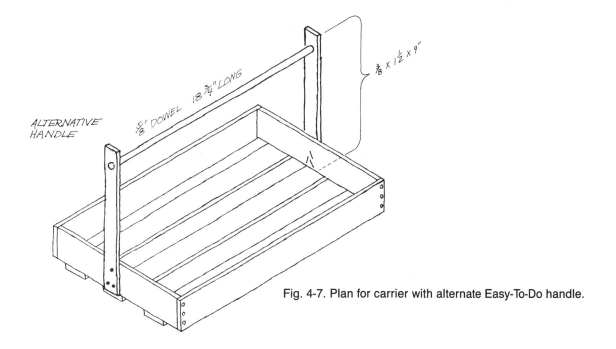

ALTERNATIVE
HANDLE

$\frac{5}{8}$" DOWEL 18 $\frac{3}{4}$" LONG

$\frac{3}{8}$ X 1 $\frac{1}{2}$ X 9"

Fig. 4-7. Plan for carrier with alternate Easy-To-Do handle.

Fig. 4-8. Empty Easy-To-Do carrier.

Fig. 4-9. Easy-To-Do style carrier with berry baskets in place and painted decoration on ends.

MATERIALS

Base—Basswood or Pine:

- 2 pieces, $3/8 \times 2^1/2 \times 11^1/4$ inches for ends
- 2 pieces, $3/8 \times 2^1/2 \times 18$ inches for sides
- 2 pieces, $3/16 \times 2^1/4 \times 18$ inches for bottom slats

Handle—Ash, Hickory, or Other Bendable Wood:

- 1 piece, $1^3/8 \times 1/4 \times 36$ inches—after bending will trim to about 32 inches.

Alternate Handle:

- 2 pieces, $3/8 \times 1^1/2 \times 9$ inches for uprights
- 1 $5/8$ inch dowel, $18^3/4$ inches long for handle

- Carpenter's glue
- Sandpaper
- Nails
- Protective varnish

CONSTRUCTION TIPS

There are different ways to bend wood to a shape, including steaming, but this method is easiest unless you have special equipment. Soak 36 inch piece of bendable wood in hot water for about 48 hours. I bind the ends of the wood with twine and tighten every few hours until I bend the wood to an arc approximately the right shape. While the wood is soaking, make a frame for drying it to shape. Draw a circle with a diameter of 18 inches on a heavy plywood board ($1/2$ inch or more thick). Then, hammer large nails ($2^1/2$ inches or larger) every inch along one of the resulting semicircles (Fig. 4-4). When the wood is flexible from soaking, place on the outside of the nails and force into place. Starting at center top, nail in place with another row of nails. Do not nail into the wood handle. Tie the ends of the wood handle together to help hold in place. Let dry for several days until completely dry. Make the base of the carrier according to the illustration in Fig. 4-3. Nail the handle to the base. Be sure to use large enough nails to deaden well on the inside of carrier (Fig. 4-5). Due to the soaking of the wood and subsequent drying, you should sand and seal with a clear, protective varnish several times before the carrier will be ready to use.

Fig. 5-1. Tray stand.

Tray Stand

Small folding tables and stands were useful in many ways in small households where floor space was limited.

The tray stand was probably used to put up a quick stand wherever needed; for instance, near a table to hold extra serving platters, etc.

Today, I use this adaptation of a nineteenth-century piece for holding luggage in the guest room. Occasionally, I also use it in the dining room to hold a large tole tray next to the table. It is a wonderful place for a large salad bowl or dessert plates and silver.

This stand has a very simple construction (Fig. 5-1). It is important to use a good, strong hardwood such as maple so it can carry a good amount of weight.

The pattern I have given for the straps is adapted from an old embroidery bell pull (Fig. 5-2). If you prefer, you can substitute a stenciled pattern or use Shaker-style strapping as used on Shaker reproduction chairs.

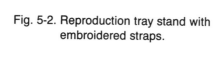

Fig. 5-2. Reproduction tray stand with embroidered straps.

MATERIALS

Wooden base: Good, clear, strong wood (maple or cherry).:

- 2 pieces, $3/4 \times 1^{1}/2 \times 20$ inches for tops
- 2 pieces, $3/4 \times 1^{1}/2 \times 34^{3}/4$ inches for legs
- 2 pieces, $3/4$-inch doweling $16^{3}/4$ inches long for braces
- 2 pieces $3/4$-inch doweling 15 inches long for braces
- 1 piece $1/2$-inch doweling $16^{3}/4$ inches long for hinge
- 1 piece $3/8$-inch doweling about 12 inches long to make plugs.
- Glue, sandpaper, paint or stain, varnish

    Straps: Enough linen or another strong material to make two straps $3^{1}/2$ inches wide and 26 inches long

- Embroidery floss or wool for working pattern
- Upholstery tacks

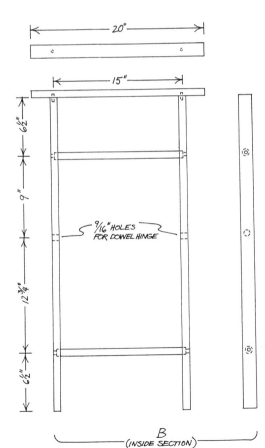

Fig. 5-3. Plan for inside section of tray stand.

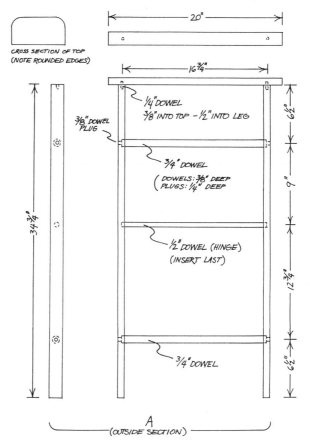

CROSS SECTION OF TOP
(NOTE ROUNDED EDGES)

20"

16¾"

¼" DOWEL
⅜" INTO TOP – ½" INTO LEG

⅜" DOWEL PLUG

¾" DOWEL

(DOWELS: ⅜" DEEP
 PLUGS: ¼" DEEP)

½" DOWEL (HINGE)
(INSERT LAST)

¾" DOWEL

34¾"

6½"

9"

12¾"

6½"

A
(OUTSIDE SECTION)

Fig. 5-4. Plan for outside section of tray stand.

CONSTRUCTION TIPS

Cut all major parts and sand (Figs. 5-3, 5-4). Drill holes for dowels and plugs. Assemble the two sides, glue, and let dry. Be careful to wipe or sand off any excess glue that oozes from holes when dowels are inserted. If you are going to stain this tray stand, it would be best to stain the wooden parts before gluing. Any glue left on the surface before staining will prevent the stain from coloring evenly. Insert dowel hinge through the holes on the narrow side. Slip the wide side over the narrow one, and by pulling legs apart, carefully slip both ends of hinge into place. Completely paint or varnish stand before tacking straps into place on the undersides (Figs. 5-5, 5-6).

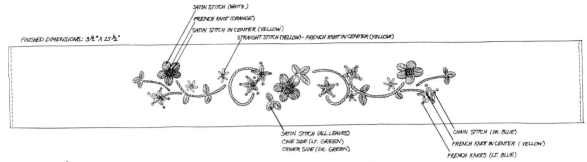

SATIN STITCH (WHITE)
FRENCH KNOT (ORANGE)
SATIN STITCH IN CENTER (YELLOW)
STRAIGHT STITCH (YELLOW) ~ FRENCH KNOT IN CENTER (YELLOW)
FINISHED DIMENSIONS: 3½" X 25½"

SATIN STITCH (ALL LEAVES)
ONE SIDE (LT. GREEN)
OTHER SIDE (DK. GREEN)

CHAIN STITCH (DK. BLUE)
FRENCH KNOT IN CENTER (YELLOW)
FRENCH KNOTS (LT. BLUE)

Fig. 5-5. Pattern for strap embroidery.

Fig. 5-6. Detail of fastening of straps.

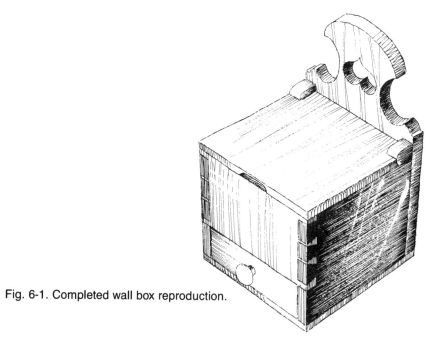

Fig. 6-1. Completed wall box reproduction.

Wall Box

Boxes of this kind were usually hung on the wall to hold salt. Salt was a very important commodity to the settlers—necessary for preserving food as well as for flavor. The salt boxes were handcrafted and varied greatly in decorative features, although they were similar in general shape and features (Fig. 6-1). If you look carefully when visiting colonial restorations, you are certain to see at least one on display.

Fig. 6-2. Wall box as originally found with lid and drawer missing.

I found the original wall box from which these plans were drawn at a local farm auction (Fig. 6-2). Buried under a pile of scraps and old, broken tools in a corner of a barn for many years, it was barely recognizable. Luckily, no one else seemed to know what it was, and I carried the treasure home. When cleaned up, the details of its careful construction were easy to see. Made entirely without nails, its dovetailing and doweling still held it together as well as when it was first crafted. The lid was gone and the little drawer broken beyond repair, but the sturdy box is evidence of the fine workmanship of the man who made it long ago (Figs. 6-3, 6-4, 6-5).

The upside-down heart is a charming aspect of this box. Often seen in early pieces from Pennsylvania, its special meaning (if indeed there was one) has long been forgotten.

This project is an excellent exercise in dovetailing and doweling. Use a soft, even-grained wood, take your time, and you will have lots of fun making it.

The original box, seen in Fig. 6-2, hangs on one of the log walls in my house and holds dried flowers to reflect the changing seasons. It is a constant delight as a conversation starter as I'm sure yours will be.

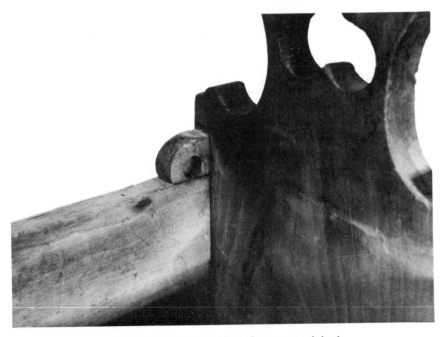

Fig. 6-3. Detail of lid hinge brace on original.

Fig. 6-4. Detail of original dovetailing.

Fig. 6-5. Back and side joining on original box.

MATERIALS

Clear, Unblemished Softwood:

- 1 piece, $3/4 \times 8^1/4 \times 12^3/4$ inches for back
- 2 pieces, $5/8 \times 6^1/2 \times 8$ inches for sides
- 1 piece, $9/16 \times 4^1/2 \times 8^1/4$ inches for front
- 1 piece, $1/2 \times 8 \times 8^1/4$ inches for lid
- 1 piece, $1/2 \times 7 \times 7^3/8$ inches for shelf
- 2 pieces, $1/2 \times 2 \times 7^5/8$ inches for drawer sides
- 1 piece, $1/2 \times 1^3/4 \times 6$ inches for drawer back
- 1 piece, $1/2 \times 2 \times 7$ inches for drawer front
- 1 piece, $1/4 \times 6^1/4 \times 7^3/8$ inches for drawer bottom
- 1 piece, $3/8 \times 8^1/4 \times 8^3/4$ inches for bottom
- 2 pieces, $5/8 \times 7/8 \times 1^3/16$ inches

- 1 wooden knob
- Carpenter's glue
- Hardwood dowels: $3/16$ inch $\times$ 3 feet
  $1/8$ inch $\times$ 2 feet

CONSTRUCTION TIPS

Note that all wood is cut to full measure and will probably have to be planed down from thicker stock. Pieces should be glued with good carpenter's glue as well as dovetailed and doweled. Close hand fitting might be necessary for the lid to move freely up and down. When doweling, groove the inner side of the dowel so that the glue will slide up the dowel and seal the joint. After inserting the dowel, cut off flush with the outside of the box and sand smooth. Rough cut all pieces. Sand flat surfaces. Cut out heart in back. Cut dovetails on front and sides. Fit and adjust until they fit well. Assemble sides and front. Put shelf in place, and dowel and glue in place. Lay box on its face. Glue back onto sides. Dowel back in place. Glue and dowel bottom in place. Sand rear edge of lid until rounded. Also round small flanges at rear of lid. See plans in Figs. 6-6 through 6-11. Make 2 section "A" pieces. Place on flanges of lid and then glue to sides as indicated. Be sure to hold all three pieces together while you do this. Assemble drawer. Rout or chisel grooves on inside of sides and front to hold the bottom of the drawer in place when the drawer is assembled. Dowel and glue drawer together as in plan. Fasten knob to center front of drawer. Put drawer into box. If you desire, this can be painted or stained, but the original was merely sanded very well and left unpainted.

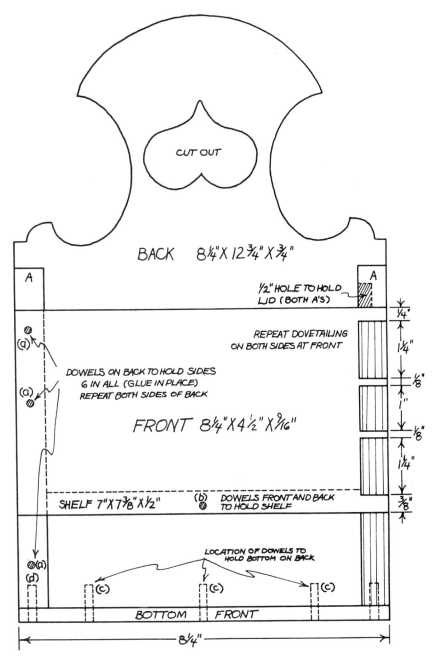

CUT OUT

BACK   8¼" X 12¾" X ¾"

A   A

½" HOLE TO HOLD
LID (BOTH A'S)

¼"

(a)   REPEAT DOVETAILING
                                                  ON BOTH SIDES AT FRONT

1¼"

⅛"

DOWELS ON BACK TO HOLD SIDES
(a)   6 IN ALL (GLUE IN PLACE)   1"
            REPEAT BOTH SIDES OF BACK

⅛"

FRONT 8¼" X 4½" X 9/16"

1¼"

SHELF 7" X 7⅞" X ½"   (b) DOWELS FRONT AND BACK   ⅜"
                                TO HOLD SHELF

LOCATION OF DOWELS TO
HOLD BOTTOM ON BACK

(a)
(d)   [(c)   [(c)   [(c)

BOTTOM   FRONT

8¼"

BOTTOM IS 8¼" X 8¾ X ⅞"   PUT ON LAST WITH 9 DOWELS (C) AS INDICATED

SHELF IS 7" X 7⅞" X ½"   HELD BY 2 DOWELS (b) AS INDICATED

NOTE: USE 3/16" DOWELING

Fig. 6-6. Front view plan.

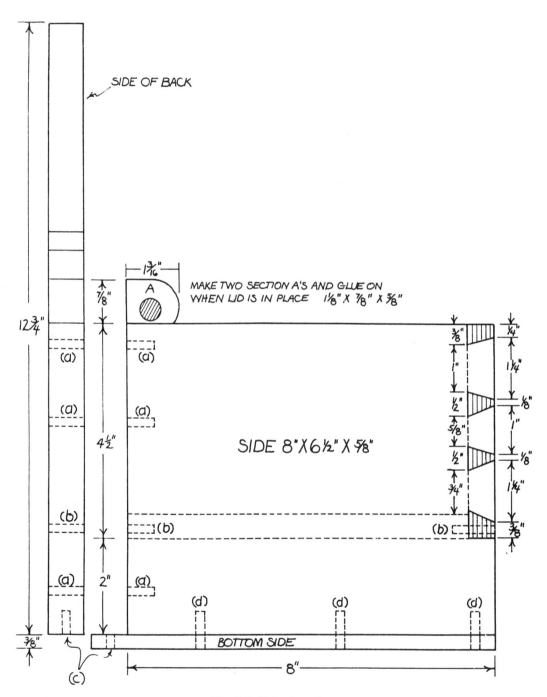

SIDE OF BACK

MAKE TWO SECTION A'S AND GLUE ON
WHEN LID IS IN PLACE   1⅛" X ⅞" X ⅝"

SIDE 8"X6½" X ⅝"

BOTTOM SIDE

Fig. 6-7. Side view plan.

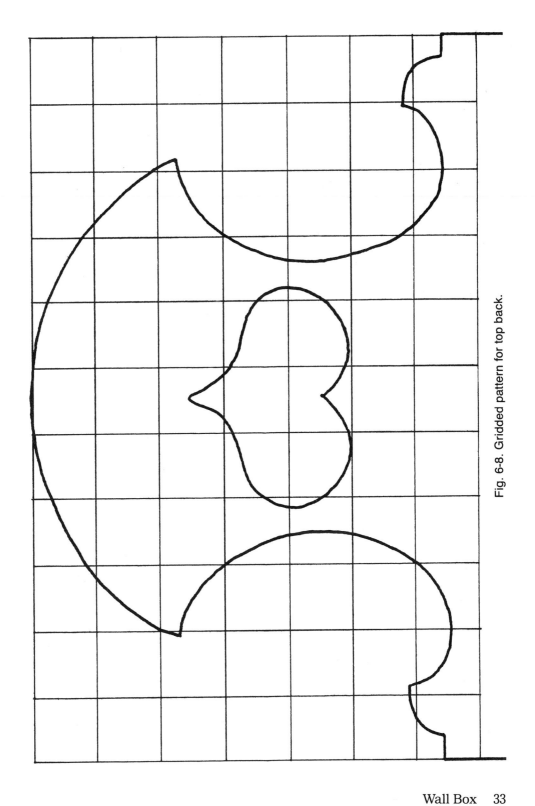

Fig. 6-8. Gridded pattern for top back.

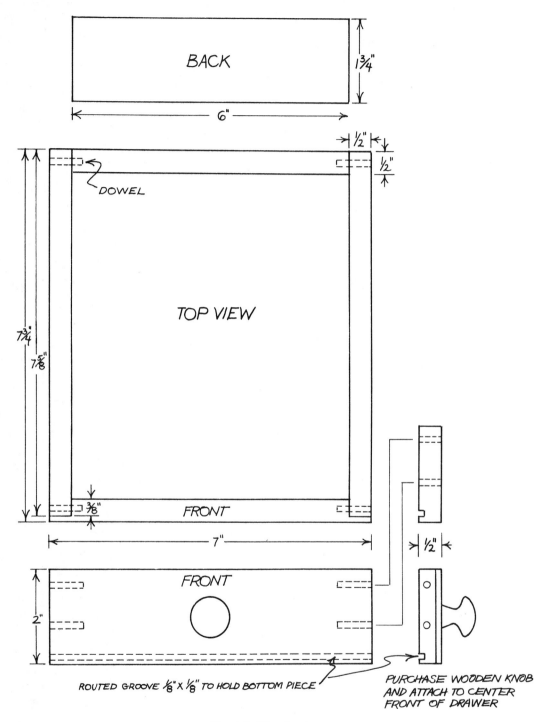

BACK

1¾"

6"

½"

½"

DOWEL

TOP VIEW

7¾"

7⅝"

⅜"

FRONT

7"

½"

FRONT

2"

ROUTED GROOVE ⅛" X ⅛" TO HOLD BOTTOM PIECE

PURCHASE WOODEN KNOB
AND ATTACH TO CENTER
FRONT OF DRAWER

Fig. 6-9. Plan for drawer.

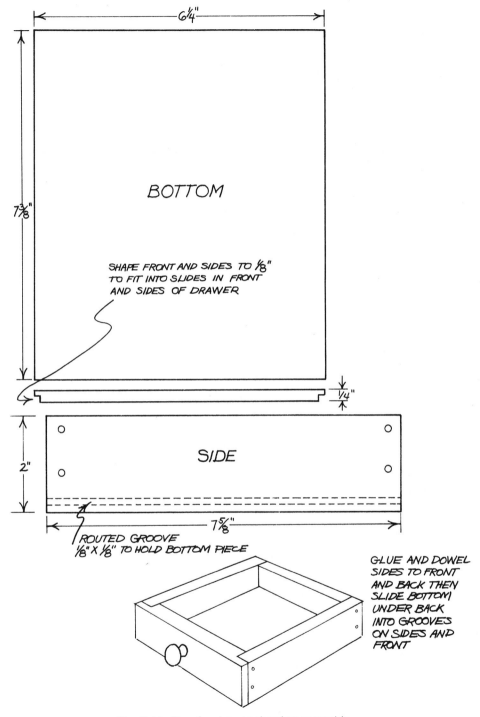

6¼"

BOTTOM

7⅜"

SHAPE FRONT AND SIDES TO ⅛"
TO FIT INTO SLIDES IN FRONT
AND SIDES OF DRAWER

¼"

SIDE

2"

7⅝"

ROUTED GROOVE
⅛" X ⅛" TO HOLD BOTTOM PIECE

GLUE AND DOWEL
SIDES TO FRONT
AND BACK THEN
SLIDE BOTTOM
UNDER BACK
INTO GROOVES
ON SIDES AND
FRONT

Fig. 6-10. Plan for drawer showing assembly.

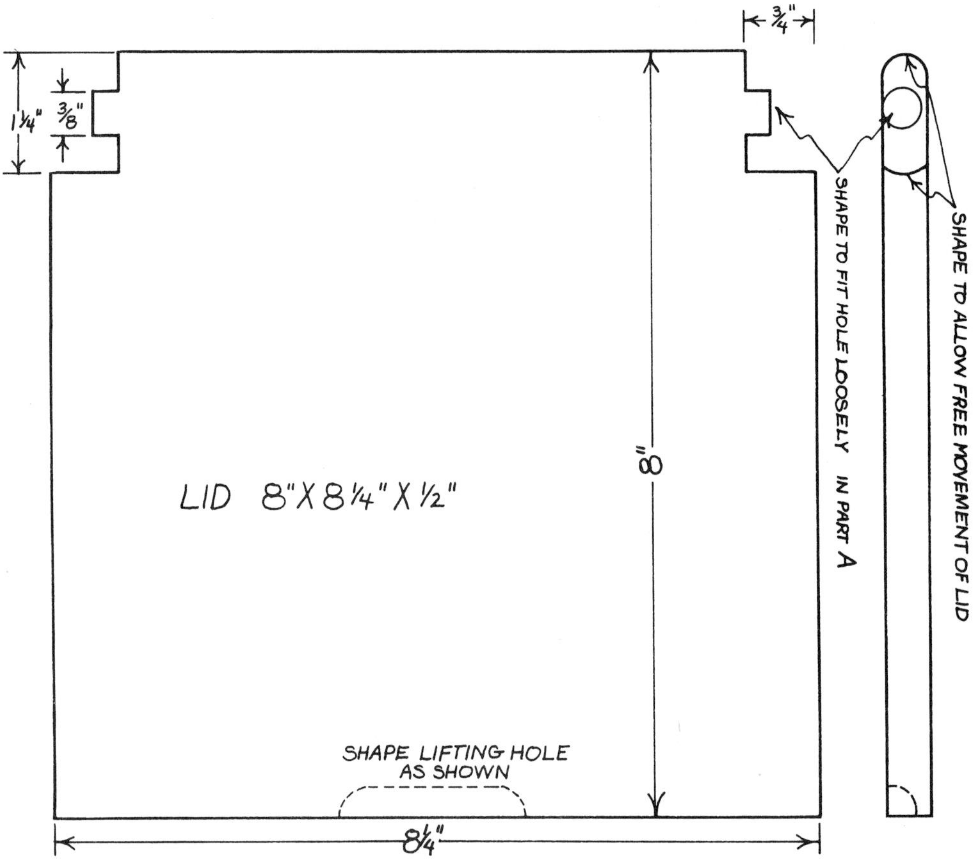

3/4"
1 1/4"
3/8"
LID 8"X8 1/4"X1/2"
8"
SHAPE TO FIT HOLE LOOSELY IN PART A
SHAPE TO ALLOW FREE MOVEMENT OF LID
SHAPE LIFTING HOLE
AS SHOWN
8 1/4"

Fig. 6-11. Plan for lid.

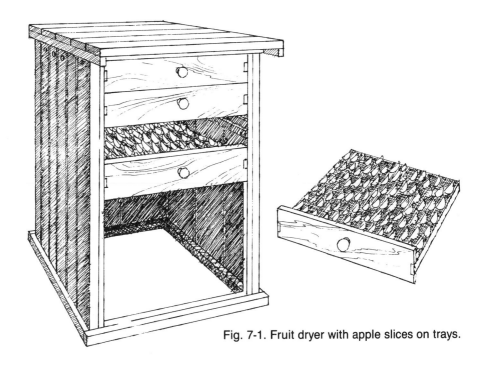

Fig. 7-1. Fruit dryer with apple slices on trays.

Fruit Dryer

Drying food was an important part of the housekeeper's duties in Early American communities. It was the best way to prepare food for keeping until the next harvest season, and it made the food easy to transport when on journeys of any length. Dried food was sometimes eaten "as is" or cooked in stews and puddings. Food that we seldom think of drying, such as pumpkins, was cut in long narrow strips and hung in barns or attics until needed. Small, whole fruits were a favorite in most homes. Larger fruits were cut in pieces. These foods were often dried in homemade dryers, on racks, or even on rocks outside.

In Japan and Nova Scotia, seaweed and fish have been dried on racks for centuries. Since drying removes the water from the food, it renders it light in weight. The dried food is easy to carry and easy to rehydrate with soaking and boiling when needed as food.

This food dryer is a sturdy adaptation of an early nineteenth-century dryer (Figs. 7-1, 7-2). Easily made, it can be knocked down for storage and reassembled when needed. It can be used with a variety of heat sources—an electric light bulb of no more than 60 watts in a porcelain socket; a small electric hot plate; or, in very dry weather, a small fan to blow air up through the trays.

If the heat source you choose is too strong or concentrated in too small an area, hang a metal baffle approximately three inches below the lowest tray to diffuse the heat.

Fig. 7-2. Reproduction fruit dryer
with one drawer open.

Old-time fruit dryers had tray frames stretched with cheesecloth, but I use nylon screening, which is easy to clean and will last longer.

The thinner the fruit or vegetables are sliced, the quicker they will dry. Slices should be turned several times during the drying process.

MATERIALS

Pine:

- $1/2 \times 3/4$ inch $\times$ 72 feet—for all framing of sides, back, top, and bottom, as well as for all drawer slides, braces, and framing for the drawers
- $1/2 \times 3$ inch $\times$ $8^{1}/2$ feet for the top
- $3/4 \times 6$ inch $\times$ 20 feet for the sides and back, enough to cover ten square feet (My wood was grooved to make the surface look more interesting).
- $1/2 \times 3$ inch $\times$ $4^{1}/2$) feet for drawer fronts
- Carpenter's glue
- Sandpaper
- Small nails—$3/4$ inch to $1^{1}/4$ inch
- One yard of 36-inch nylon screening
- Tacks or staples to fasten screening to drawer frames
- 4 wood or porcelain drawer pulls

CONSTRUCTION TIPS

Sides

Cut four pieces $1/2 \times 3/4 \times 23^{3}/4$ inches, and four pieces $1/2 \times 3/4 \times 15^{1}/2$ inches for framing the sides. Cut sixteen pieces $1/2 \times 3/4 \times 14$ inches for slides and braces. Cut enough $3/4$-inch thick siding $23^{3}/4$ inches long to cover sides (Figs. 7-3 through 7-6).

Back

Cut two pieces $1/2 \times 3/4 \times 12^3/4$ for top and bottom frame. Nail siding to these. Cut siding $23^3/4$ inches long to cover sides and back. Assemble frames with lap joints as shown in Fig. 7-6. Glue and nail joints, then nail siding to the frames. Glue and nail slides and braces to the sides (see Fig. 7-6). Drill $3/4$-inch holes for ventilation in sides at top.

Bottom Frame

Cut two pieces $1/2 \times 3/4 \times 16^1/4$ inches for front and back. Cut two pieces $1/2 \times 3/4 \times 16^1/2$ inches for sides. Cut one piece $1/2 \times 3/4 \times 12^3/4$ inches for front brace (Fig. 7-3). Assemble with lap joints, and glue and nail. Nail brace to center inside front. Notice frame will sit on $1/2$ inch of stock.

Framing and Braces for Top

Cut two pieces $1/2 \times 3/4 \times 17^1/2$ inches for sides at corners with back piece. Cut one piece $1/2 \times 3/4 \times 16^1/4$ inches for back. Cut one piece $1/2 \times 3/4 \times 15^1/4$ inches for brace. Cut two pieces $1/2 \times 3/4 \times 14^1/4$ inches for side of inner frame. Cut one piece $1/2 \times 3/4 \times 11^1/4$ inches for back of inner frame. Do not lap with sides.

Top

Assemble with lap joints on back of outer frame only. Cut enough $1/2 \times 3 \times 17^1/2$ inch pieces to cover top. Glue and nail together to form top. Note: The top and bottom frame should hold entire dryer steady when sides and back are placed into them.

Drawers

Cut four pieces $1/2 \times 3 \times 12^3/4$ inches for front. Cut eight pieces $1/2 \times 3/4 \times 14$ inches for sides. Cut four pieces $1/2 \times 3/4 \times 12^1/4$ inches for backs. Cut four pieces $1/2 \times 3/4 \times 11^3/4$ inches for braces behind drawer fronts to hold screening. Make joints as on plan. Note: The $11^3/4$-inch brace fits between sides and is nailed to the back of the drawer front. Tack nylon screening to the top of the drawer frames. Fasten drawer pulls.

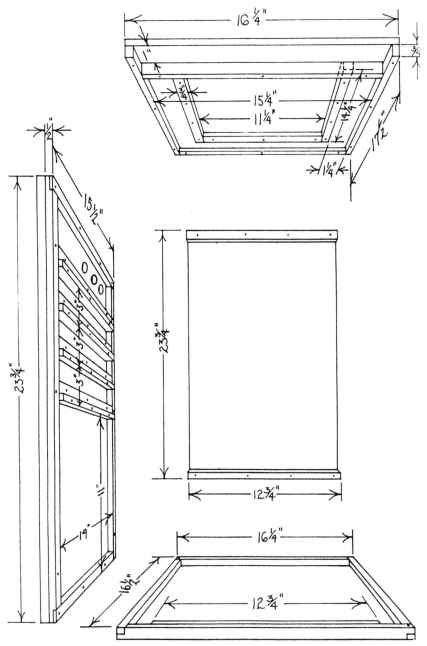

Fig. 7-3. Exploded view plan for dryer body.

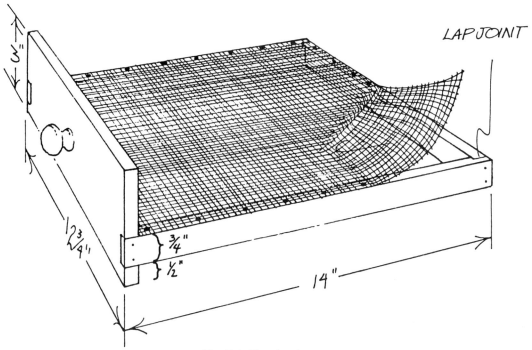

Fig. 7-4. Plan for drawer.

Fig. 7-5. Top view of drawer construction.

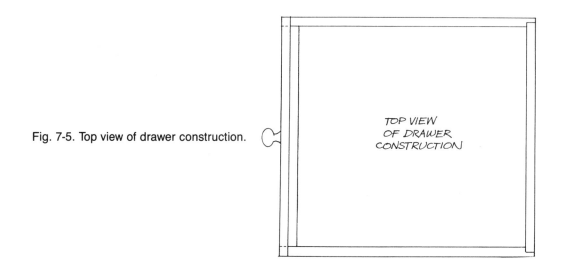

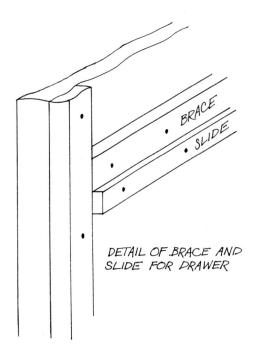

Fig. 7-6. Detail of brace and slide for drawer.

DETAIL OF BRACE AND
SLIDE FOR DRAWER

PART 2

Furniture

Country classic furniture as depicted in this book consists of the wonderful, simple, utilitarian pieces handcrafted by early settlers from wood they cut from native forests. Furniture of a more sophisticated and refined style was brought from Europe to our coastal settlements by the well-to-do. American cabinet-makers using the native woods copied the European styles in simplified form. These pieces were copied in turn by unschooled rural craftsmen in settlements further west.

When the frontier moved inland from the coast, it was increasingly difficult for the pioneers to take furniture with them. After reaching their destination, the pioneer householder built his log or sod shelter and then the necessary furnishings for its interior. These early functional pieces are sturdy, uncluttered, and durable like the men who made them. Much of the charm and individuality of these country pieces is due to the conditions and manner by which they were produced. Each piece reveals much about the craftsman, the tools he used, and the native environment in which he lived. When authentic early furniture is studied carefully, the scribe marks for joining, the marks of the axe and plane, and little miscuts come to view. The aptitude of the woodworker in choosing and cutting wood as well as his skill with tools can often be read in the tell-tale signs left for us to interpret.

Country furniture was made in all parts of rural America in the seventeenth, eighteenth, and nineteenth centuries. Craftsmen building with their fathers' methods made pieces that are sometimes difficult to date. Often the finishing methods or decorations are a clue to when the piece was constructed. The heritage of the families who first owned an early piece can also often be revealed by the decorations used. The Pennsylvania Dutch and Swedish immigrants brought traditional colors and designs with them and applied them to furniture they made here in the colonies. Other groups wishing to have their furniture look more like that of their homelands painted wood grains or marbled the surface of the plain, softwoods of their American-made pieces.

Seeking the background of an antique is like a detective search with each bit of information leading to the next. Studying an old bench or table and making a reproduction following the old methods brings you closer to our rich early history and the people who contributed to our country's settlement. The men who established this land were brave, tough, and persistent, and their character is reflected in the country furniture that has endured to enrich us all.

Fig. 8-1. Peg shelf rack.

Shelf Peg Rack

In the homes of early settlers, there were no clothes closets. The family sometimes stored clothing in blanket chests, trunks, or in freestanding wardrobes, but the usual arrangement was to hang clothing on pegs. The pegs were often driven directly into the walls or doors. Other times they were fashioned into peg boards that were fastened to the wall.

Shaker communities used peg boards that spanned the room from wall to wall about five or six feet above the floor. The Shakers used these pegs to hang all sorts of articles and keep them out of the way. The custom was to hang chairs in this manner when they were not in use, thus leaving the floors uncluttered.

The lack of closets in early homes was not the great inconvenience it would be for today's families because the settlers had very few clothes. One set of daily garments and one set of ''go to meeting'' clothes were the usual for early colonists.

This rack is a typical Pennsylvania Dutch shelf with pegs. It is embellished with a cut-out heart and curving supports (Figs. 8-1, 8-2). If you rout a groove lengthwise on the top of the shelf about an inch from the back edge, plates can be displayed on it. This rack can be stained to blend with Victorian decor or can be painted or left unfinished to fit a more rustic setting.

Fig. 8-2. Reproduction peg shelf rack.

MATERIALS

Wood:

- 2 pieces, 1 × 4$\frac{1}{2}$ × 6$\frac{1}{4}$ inches for brackets
- 1 piece, 1 × 5$\frac{1}{2}$ × 67 inches for back
- 1 piece, 1 × 7$\frac{1}{2}$ × 67 inches for shelf
- 10 hardwood pegs about three inches long, or make them from dowels with a diameter of $\frac{1}{2}$ inch
- 4 mounting screws to fasten to wall
- Sandpaper and glue
- Paint, stain, varnish
- Wooden plugs or plastic wood to fill screw holes

CONSTRUCTION TIPS

Cut pattern of shelf back and brackets (Figs. 8-3 through 8-7). Sand. Cut groove along top of shelf. Use router or chisel. Cut heart design in back and drill holes for pegs. The size of the hole you drill is determined by the size of your pegs. Glue and screw brackets to back. Countersink screws. Glue pegs in holes. Glue and nail shelf onto back and brackets. Sand and paint or stain; varnish. Drill holes through back for mounting screws. Countersink screws. After fastening shelf to wall, fill holes with wooden plugs or plastic wood. Sand and stain or paint.

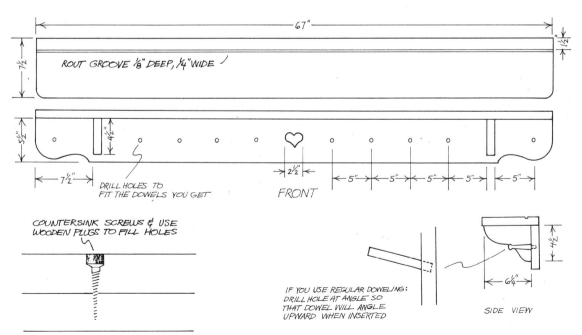

Fig. 8-3. Overall plan for rack.

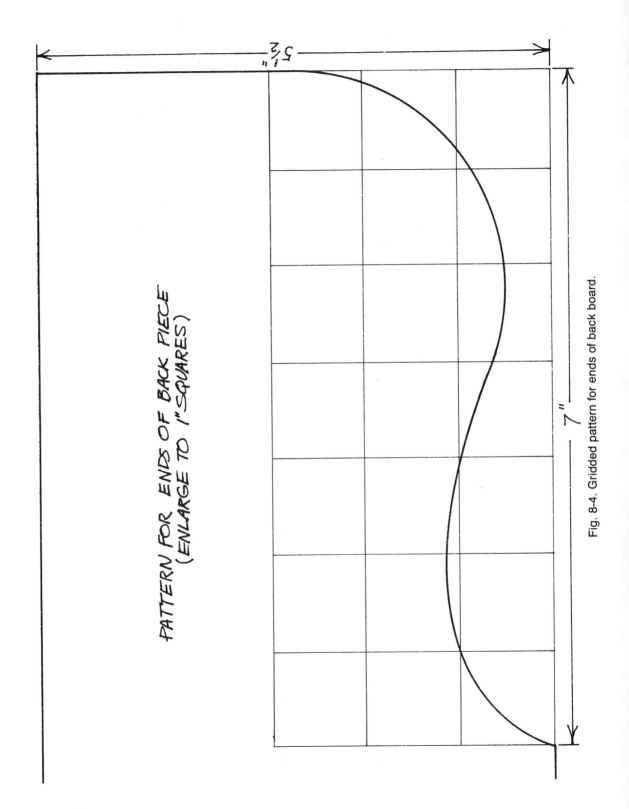

PATTERN FOR ENDS OF BACK PIECE
(ENLARGE TO 1" SQUARES)

5½"

7"

Fig. 8-4. Gridded pattern for ends of back board.

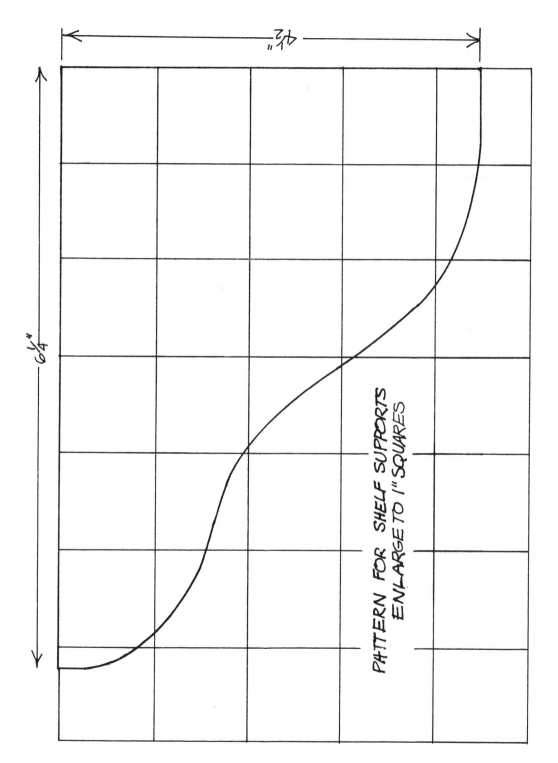

PATTERN FOR SHELF SUPPORTS
ENLARGE TO 1" SQUARES

4½"

6¼"

Fig. 8-5. Gridded pattern for shelf supports.

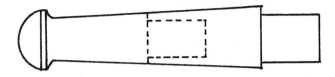

PEGS BOUGHT OR MADE

2 SIZES SHOWN (FULL SIZE)

Fig. 8-6. Pattern for pegs.

HEART PATTERN

(FULL SIZE)

Fig. 8-7. Pattern for cut-out heart.

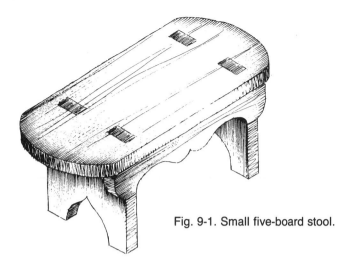

Fig. 9-1. Small five-board stool.

Small Five-Board Stool

The original mideighteenth-century footstool from which this pattern was adapted is in Massachusetts. Meticulously made by some unknown craftsman, its rounded top, mortised joints, Gothic ogee legs, and curving sideboard make it a gem among footstools (Fig. 9-1).

The original footstool has a grey-green, painted underbody. The top might once have been painted, but the paint is completely worn off. It is a tiny footstool and perhaps was intended for use by a child (Fig. 9-2).

Fig. 9-2. Unfinished reproduction stool.

Footstools of this type were a common household item in early times and were made in all sizes. Known as five-board stools, they had many uses. Children used them as seats, and adults used them to climb into their high beds, to rest their feet on, and to stand on to reach high shelves. Each craftsman, who was often the rural householder himself, developed his own style of stool, but almost all had three main parts—the top, the legs, and the side braces that held the stool together.

This stool is fun to make, and if you want an easy-to make version, eliminate the mortises and tenons.

Whichever plan you use, the footstool will be charming. I like the unfinished top with the painted underbody, as the original is now, but finish according to your own taste. A milk-based paint would be perfect, but any matte finish in early colors such as barn red, grey-green, or mustard would be attractive and true to the period.

MATERIALS

Pine or Maple:

- 1 piece, $3/4 \times 6^1/2 \times 14^1/2$ inches for top
- 2 pieces, $3/4 \times 1^7/8 \times 11$ inches for aprons
- 2 pieces, $3/4 \times 6^1/4 \times 6^1/2$ inches for legs

- Carpenter's glue
- Sandpaper
- Finishing nails
- Paint or stain, and varnish, if desired

CONSTRUCTION TIPS

Rough cut all five pieces and sand (Figs. 9-3, 9-4). Cut mortises in top as follows; mark pattern for mortises. Drill several holes within mortise area. Use keyhole saw and straight-edge rasp to fine-finish cutting. (A chisel can be used instead of a keyhole saw, but be careful not to damage sides of mortise rectangular hole. Fit tenons into mortises. They should fit snugly, so sand and trim a little at a time until they are perfect. Glue tenons into mortises. Glue and nail aprons into place on legs. Countersink nails and fill holes. Sand top of tenons until flush with rest of top. Sand overall. Sand edge of top until it is slightly rounded. Place stool on perfectly flat surface. If it does not stand square, sand or cut bottom of legs until it is square. The stool is ready to finish as you wish with paint or stain.

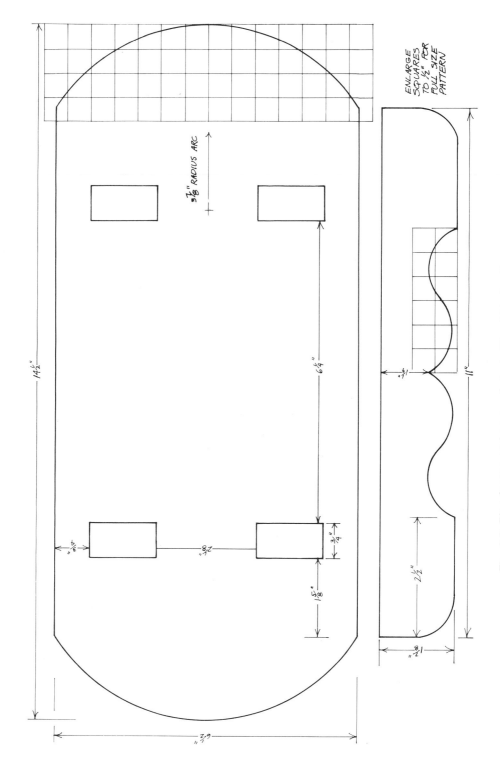

Fig. 9-3. Plan for top and apron of stool with gridded pattern on curves.

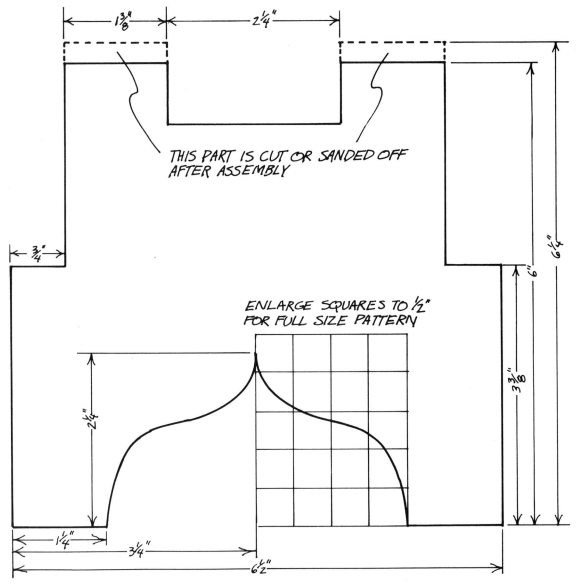

THIS PART IS CUT OR SANDED OFF AFTER ASSEMBLY

ENLARGE SQUARES TO ½" FOR FULL SIZE PATTERN

Fig. 9-4. Plan for leg sections of five-board stool with gridded pattern on curves.

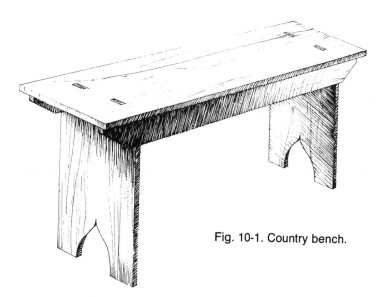

Fig. 10-1. Country bench.

Country Bench

Benches were the usual seating furniture in pioneer homes as they were easily made from native wood and simple tools. Early schools, inns, churches, and farms put benches to good use. They were made in all sizes from two feet to twenty feet in length. At first, most benches were fashioned with straight boards and legs cut with a simple upside-down "V." As craftsmen had a little more time and perhaps better tools, the designs became somewhat more sophisticated with shaped aprons and Gothic ogees cut in the sides to make the legs.

This double-aproned mortised bench has been a perennial favorite in all parts of rural America (Fig. 10-1). Typical of rural benches made over a century ago, it is still a popular necessity in the farm country of Pennsylvania, where they are used for social gatherings and religious meetings.

Old benches can still be found at auctions and in antique shops but at a steep price, so why not try making your own "future antique?" (Fig. 10-2).

If you don't want to try making the mortise and tenons, use my Easy-to-Do plan in Figs. 10-5 and 10-6. Many early benches were made this way, so your bench will still be authentic in design.

I like the bench either painted or left unfinished except for a protective coat. If you want to stencil or paint in Pennsylvania folk art fashion on the aprons or legs, use a good matte-finish paint in grey-green or blue for a base color. Painted furniture, Pennsylvania Dutch style, was much more popular in Pennsylvania than in other parts of America. This was probably due to the German-Swiss background of the Pennsylvania settlers who copied the seventeenth-century furniture of their homelands.

However you finish your bench, I'm sure you will find many uses for it in your home.

Fig. 10-2. Antique bench that was never painted.

MATERIALS

Pine, Poplar, Maple, or Walnut:

- 2 pieces, $3/4 \times 11^3/8 \times 21$ inches for leg sections. The finished piece will be shorter, but allow more length for tenon, which is cut or sanded off after being fit into the mortise.
- 2 pieces, $5/8 \times 3 \times 46$ inches for aprons
- 1 piece, $5/8 \times 13^3/8 \times 48$ inches for seat. This pattern calls for the width of the original, and the lumber can be difficult to find. It can be made from smaller boards glued and clamped, but first try home-building supply houses, as they sometimes have pieces already made for large shelving or table tops.

- Sandpaper and carpenter's glue
- Varnish or paint

CONSTRUCTION TIPS

Mortising this bench is somewhat tricky (see Figs. 10-3 through 10-6). Cut out and finish sanding the leg sections first, leaving the tenons long, as noted on the plans. Turning the leg sections upside down on the upside-down seat, trace the tenons, and mark the places where the mortise slots are to be cut out. Be very careful to cut these slots narrower than traced to ensure that the tenons fit snugly. I cut the slots by drilling several holes through the seat and then finishing with a straight chisel and a 90-degree corner chisel. Sand and trim a little at a time until the tenon fits exactly as desired, then glue in place.

When glue is set, trim off the part of the tenon that extends out of the seat until it is flush. (This extension will probably be out of shape from forcing into the mortise slot.) Note: If a tenon is too loose in the slot, you can cut diagonally through to the base, replace into the slot, and wedge with a small hardwood wedge (Fig. 10-4). All sections of the bench are glued. The apron is also nailed or pegged to the legs.

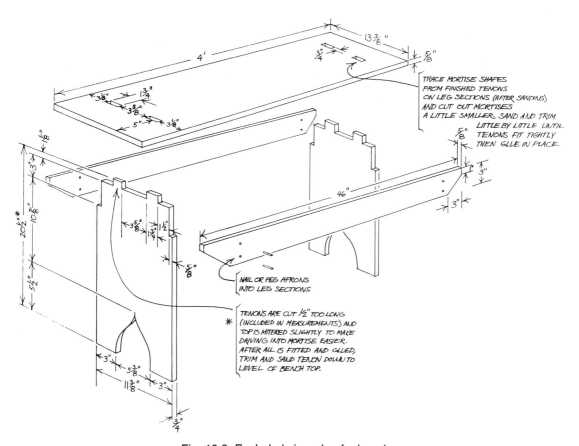

Fig. 10-3. Exploded view plan for bench.

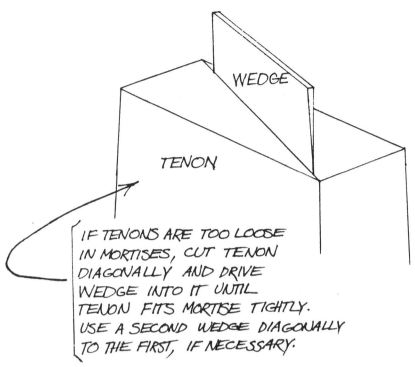

WEDGE

TENON

IF TENONS ARE TOO LOOSE
IN MORTISES, CUT TENON
DIAGONALLY AND DRIVE
WEDGE INTO IT UNTIL
TENON FITS MORTISE TIGHTLY.
USE A SECOND WEDGE DIAGONALLY
TO THE FIRST, IF NECESSARY.

Fig. 10-4. Diagram showing how tenons are wedged.

Fig. 10-5. Detail of brace added when mortises and
tenons are eliminated as in Easy-To-Do plan.

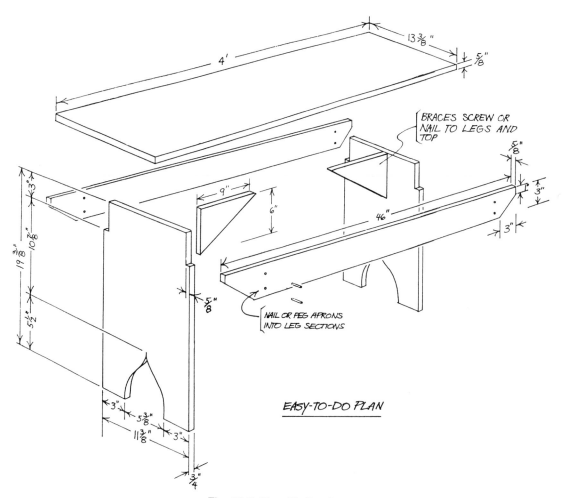

13 3/8 "

4'

5/8"

BRACES SCREW OR
NAIL TO LEGS AND
TOP

5/8"

3"

9"

6"

46"

3"

3"

3"

10 8/8"

19 3/8"

5/8"

5 1/2"

NAIL OR PEG APRONS
INTO LEG SECTIONS

EASY-TO-DO PLAN

3"

5 3/8"

3"

11 3/8"

3/4"

Fig. 10-6. Easy-To-Do plan.

Fig. 11-1. Dust free plate rack.

Dust-Free Plate Rack

This plate rack is copied from an early Pennsylvania piece that I saw, photographed, and measured in an old stone farmhouse in central Pennsylvania (Figs. 11-1, 11-2). The family who owned it had a real treasure house of early pieces, but this was one of my favorites. The first reproduction of the rack hangs in my living room along with many antiques, and it fits in beautifully holding old pewter and Wedgwood plates (Fig. 11-3).

Fig. 11-2. Antique plate rack in room setting where found.

Fig. 11-3. Reproduction in use.

The outstanding feature of this style of rack gives it its name. Plates slant downward, face forward, when properly placed on its shelves. It is called a *dust-free plate rack* because dust and ashes fall on the backs of the plates, leaving the faces of the plates clean and ready to use. As these plates were often in kitchens or *keeping rooms* where fireplaces burned constantly, this feature was very important to the busy housewife in early America.

The first plate racks made in this country might have been copied from ones early craftsmen had seen in France. Even today, racks of this type are occasionally seen in French country homes.

The curvature of the sides and the large dovetail joints combine to make this piece very attractive, especially when hung on an all-white wall. Three feet, six and a half inches wide, and two feet, two inches high, it holds up to a dozen plates of different sizes, with the largest on the top shelf. All the parts are straight boards except for the shaped sides. Measurements are for the finished pieces except the sides, which must be cut following the plan. I suggest you use pine and cherry as in the original.

As you can see in Fig. 11-8, early craftsmen often made mistakes just as we do. The groove for the brace in one side was cut too large or perhaps in the wrong position. Instead of filling in or making a whole new side, the craftsman recut the groove and left the scar.

MATERIALS

Pine:

- 2 pieces, $3/4 \times 31/2$ inches $\times$ 3 feet 6 inches for shelves
- 2 pieces, $3/4 \times 81/2$ inches $\times$ 2 feet 2 inches for sides
- 1 piece, $3/4 \times 81/2$ inches $\times$ 3 feet 7 inches for top board
- 1 piece, $3/4 \times 31/2$ inches $\times$ 3 feet 7 inches for bottom board
- 1 piece, $1/2 \times 3/4$ inches $\times$ 3 feet 51/2 inches for edge on bottom of front board

Cherry or Maple:

- Three pieces, $5/8 \times 11/2$ inches $\times$ 3 feet 6 inches for braces

Iron:

- 2 hangers, $1/2 \times 3$ inches with small holes at one end for screws and large hole at top. These are to mount on rear top of sides in order to hang rack on wall.

- Carpenter's glue and sandpaper
- Stain, if desired
- Varnish

CONSTRUCTION TIPS

Rough cut all pieces and sand (Figs. 11-4 through 11-7). Try a couple of dovetail joints in a scrap or wood. When you feel confident, start on the actual project. You can make the large dovetail joints on this project with a coping saw, mallet, and chisel. Use a rasp to smooth the sides. Cut dovetails in the sides first; then, holding them tight against the top, trace the pattern with a sharp knife or pencil. Cut a little at a time, carefully fitting and sanding until you get a close fit. Repeat for bottom board. Cut grooves with router or chisel on inside of both side boards as indicated on plan. These grooves should be $1/4$ of an inch deep. If desired, route or chisel groove on top of each shelf about $1/8$ of an inch from rear. This should be about $1/8$ of an inch deep and $1/8$ to $1/4$ of an inch in width. Fit all pieces together, trimming and sanding until everything goes together well. The fit should be fairly tight. Take apart. Sand and stain all pieces. Put together again and glue all pieces together and clamp until dry. Wipe with tack cloth and stain, varnish, or wax as desired. Attach hangers to top of sides.

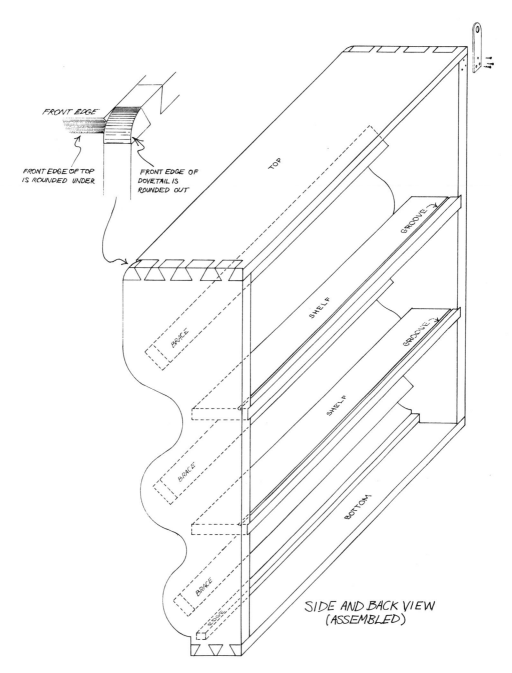

FRONT EDGE

FRONT EDGE OF TOP
IS ROUNDED UNDER

FRONT EDGE OF
DOVETAIL IS
ROUNDED OUT

TOP

GROOVE

SHELF

BRACE

GROOVE

SHELF

BRACE

BOTTOM

BRACE

SIDE AND BACK VIEW
(ASSEMBLED)

Fig. 11-4. Plan and assembly for rack.

Dust-Free Plate Rack   63

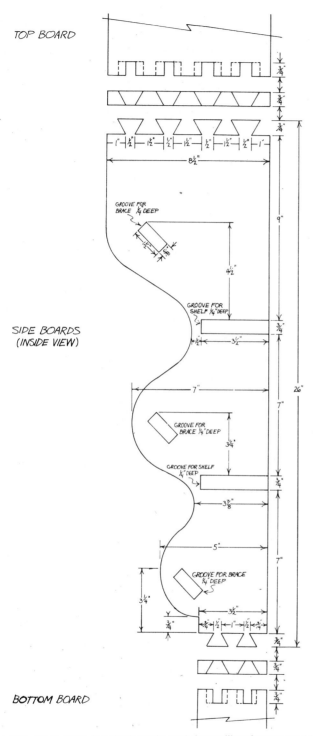

Fig. 11-5. Plan for sideboards and dovetailing for top and bottom boards.

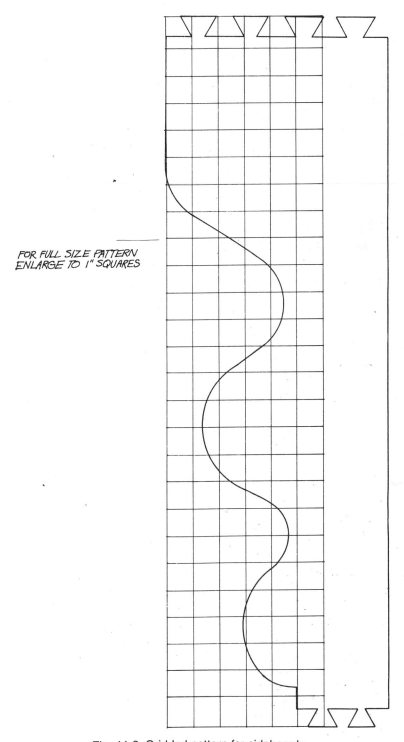

FOR FULL SIZE PATTERN
ENLARGE TO 1" SQUARES

Fig. 11-6. Gridded pattern for sideboards.

Fig. 11-7. Detail of dovetailing at bottom.

Fig. 11-8. Detail showing miscut on original antique.

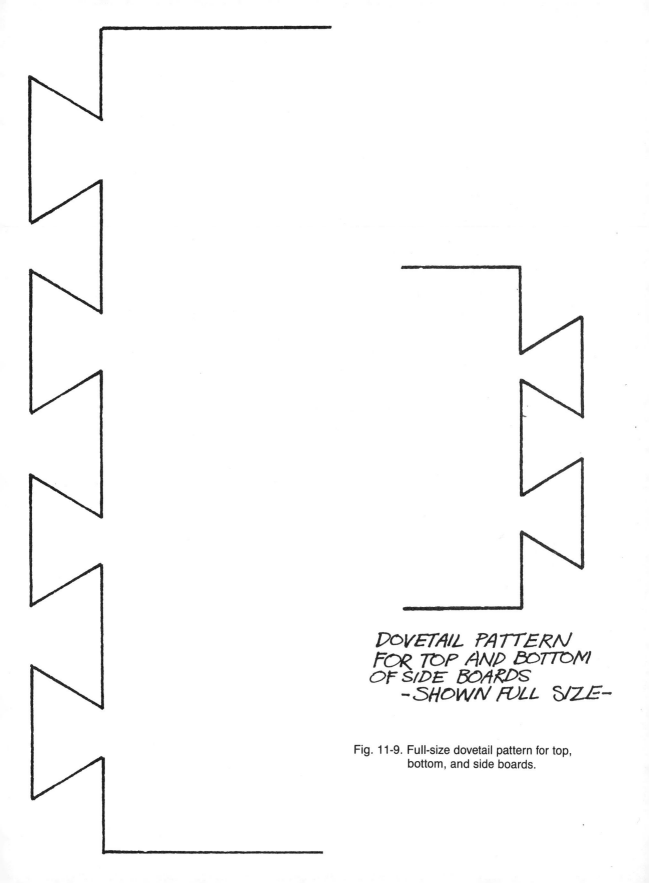

DOVETAIL PATTERN
FOR TOP AND BOTTOM
OF SIDE BOARDS
—SHOWN FULL SIZE—

Fig. 11-9. Full-size dovetail pattern for top,
bottom, and side boards.

Fig. 11-10. Detail of bottom front of antique.

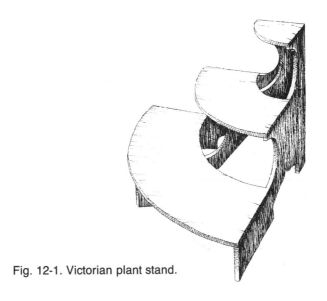

Fig. 12-1. Victorian plant stand.

Victorian Plant Stand

Called *etagere a fleurs* in France, plant stands like this one enjoyed a vogue in America as the nineteenth century progressed and more and more houses had sun rooms and solariums. Some, like this one, were utilitarian; they were simple backgrounds for displaying plants and flowers. Others, in the hands of Victorian artisans, were embellished with enough intricate flourishes to become major decorative pieces in their own right.

Fig. 12-2. Reproduction plant stand that is painted dark green.

This stand is a quarter-round, and fits into a corner (Figs. 12-1, 12-2). Four units like this can be used as a free-standing circular display. The pattern can also be adapted to make a rectangular unit to fit along a straight wall. To do this, simply make all the ends and supports by pattern A, and use straight shelving of the needed length. Straight braces can be placed at the back where necessary. Painted with a dark green-black paint, either stand will be a perfect foil for your plants.

MATERIALS

Pine:

- Clear board, $5/8 \times 23^{1}/_{4} \times 132$ inches—or use 2 boards, one 60 inches long, one 72 inches long. If you cannot find boards of these dimensions, use good grade plywood finished on both sides. Finish edges with trim glued to edges.
- 1 piece, $2 \times 2 \times 15$ inches for corner brace (D).
- Screws, three or four 1-inch screws for attaching part A to part B.
- Finishing nails
- Wood filler
- Sandpaper and carpenter's glue
- Wood sealer
- Good quality enamel paint

CONSTRUCTION TIPS

Make a full-size paper pattern of all pieces (Fig. 12-5). Lay out the pattern on the wood to avoid any splits or knotholes at the edges of the shelves and major pieces (Figs. 12-3, 12-4). Trace and cut out all pieces. The inner edge of C will have to be mitered to fit into the 90-degree angle formed by A and B when joined. One corner of brace D must be cut along the 15-inch length until the diagonal measure into the corner is 2 inches. See top view sketch (Fig. 12-6).

Drill holes for screws. Glue and screw A to B. Countersink screws, fill with wood filler, and let dry. Sand smooth. Make certain A and B make a 90-degree angle when joined (Figs. 12-6, 12-7, 12-8). Glue and nail brace D into the corner flush with floor. Glue and nail section C in place with the notched part resting firmly on the brace. Trim and sand until these sections set squarely on level floor. Refit shelves, trimming supports if necessary. Glue and nail shelves in place. Resand. Fill all screw and nail holes and sand.

Apply sanding sealer to the entire piece, including inside areas. Let dry and sand smooth. Apply a second coat of sealer if needed, let dry, and sand. Paint with a good quality enamel, using two or three coats, drying and sanding between each. A plastic finish can be applied over the enamel, if desired, for an extra durable finish.

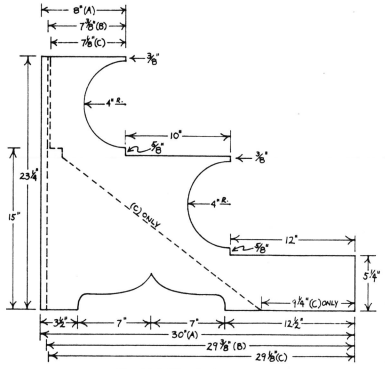

Fig. 12-3. Plan for leg supports.

Fig. 12-4. Plan for steps.

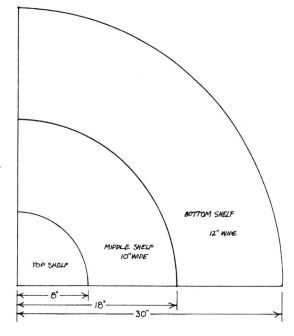

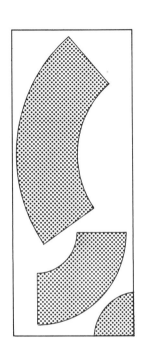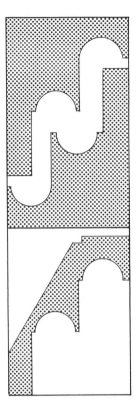

Fig. 12-5. Suggested pattern layout.

SUGGESTED PATTERN LAYOUT

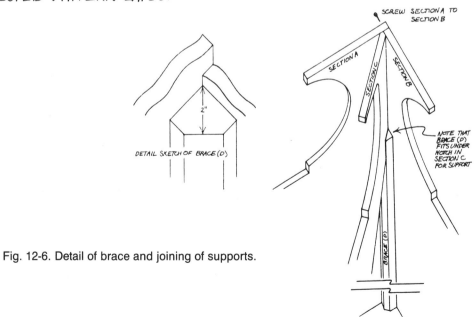

2"

DETAIL SKETCH OF BRACE (D)

SCREW SECTION A TO SECTION B

SECTION A

SECTION C

SECTION B

NOTE THAT BRACE (D) FITS UNDER NOTCH IN SECTION C FOR SUPPORT

BRACE (D)

Fig. 12-6. Detail of brace and joining of supports.

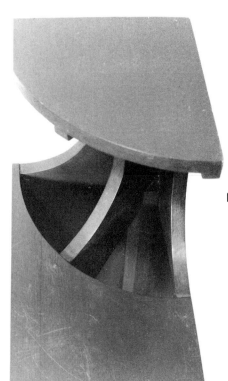

Fig. 12-7. Detail of top of stand.

Fig. 12-8. Detail showing center leg support.

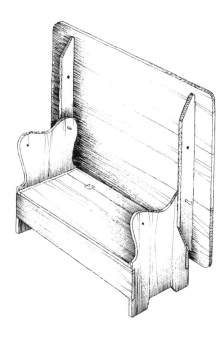

Fig. 13-1. Settle table with top tilted back to make a seat.

Settle Table

Settle tables are an excellent example of convertible furniture made by woodworkers in the late 1700s and 1800s. Intended to use available space as efficiently as possible, they were used in keeping rooms, which seemed to have functioned as combination kitchen/family rooms in early homesteads. In fact, in many rural homes there was only one room and perhaps a sleeping loft. Every piece of furniture had to be as useful as possible. Chests were used as seats as well as for storing things and were sometimes even slept upon. Trundle beds were pushed out of the way under big beds, and the settle table was a seat, a table, and a storage area. Many of these early American items would be useful for present-day apartment owners if they could find old ones or make reproductions themselves.

When open fireplaces were the only source of warmth in homes, people sat close to the hearth. The fire warmed the front of a person, but drafts chilled the back and neck. Thus the popularity of the settle bench. When turned up to make a seat, the table top was high enough to protect the back and neck, and the sides afforded protection to the rest of the body (Fig. 13-1). These settles, when used as a bench, were generally designed to seat two or three. Often they had boxes with hinged tops as seats, and sometimes drawers were fastened under the seats. The boxes were made to hold the family Bibles that often contained the only record of family history such as births, deaths, and marriages.

Hutch or *settle tables*, as they are called, are found in many of the native American woods including pine, maple, poplar, and cherry. The legs (side

Fig. 13-2. Original settle table with top down in table position.

pieces) were of the stronger woods, and the holding pins for the top were usually of hardwood. It was common for the early furniture maker to use different woods in one piece as his purpose was primarily utilitarian.

The top of this type of table can be either rectangular or round, and there can be a storage area or a drawer. The outstanding feature of all these tables is the way the top swings up to make a seat and down to form a table. This flexibility is provided by the four holding pegs. When all four pegs are inserted through the table top's braces into the leg sections, the top is as firm and steady as a table. By removing two pegs along the front side of the seat, the top can be swung backward to make a high-backed seat.

I have seen many of these old settles in many styles, but my own from early New England is still my favorite, and I have made these plans from it (Fig. 13-2). The table will serve as a table for six (or eight, if some are children), and the storage area holds most of my tablecloths and place mats. I hope you will enjoy owning your own settle bench.

MATERIALS

You might have to glue and blind-dowel stock together in order to get the various widths necessary for this project. If you cannot find full 1-inch-thick wood, you can substitute 3/4-inch thick (which is generally referred to as one inch) for the various parts that make up the box. Be sure to make the necessary changes in cuts in the sides if you do change the thickness of the wood for the box.

Wood:

- 1 piece, $1 \times 38 \times 53^{1/2}$ inches for the table top (Part A).
- 2 pieces, $1 \times 18 \times 28^{1/2}$ inches for the sides (Part B).
- 2 pieces, $1 \times 9 \times 37^{1/2}$ inches for the sides of the box (Part C).
- 1 piece, $1 \times 15 \times 34^{1/2}$ inches for movable lid of box (Part D).
- 1 piece, $1 \times 16^{3/4} \times 35^{1/2}$ inches for bottom of box (Part E).
- 2 pieces, $1 \times 1 \times 14$ inches for fixed sides of top of box (Part F).
- 1 piece, $1 \times 3^{1/2} \times 36^{1/2}$ inches for fixed lid of box (Part G).
- 2 pieces, $1 \times 3^{1/2} \times 36$ inches for table top supports (Part H).

- 4 hinge pins of hardwood
- Screws of various lengths and wooden plugs to cover them
- 2 hinges for lid of box
- Large furniture clamps
- Sandpaper and carpenter's glue
- Finish paint or varnish

CONSTRUCTION TIPS

Cut parts to size and sand. Cut dado into inner sides of part B with chisel or router. These grooves support fixed lid parts F and G. Drill holes in part B for hinge pins (Fig. 13-3). Cut grooves $3/8$-inch deep by one-inch high in part C to support part E (Fig. 13-5). Glue bottom of box (part E) in place (Fig. 13-5). Secure with countersunk screws through part B where indicated on plan. Glue and fasten sides of box (part C) to sides (part B). Glue support blocks under long edges of bottoms to reinforce where part E joins part C (Fig. 13-5). Glue fixed parts of top (parts F and G) in dado and to top edge of rear (part C) (Fig. 13-5). Curve front edge of movable lid (part D) by sanding (Fig. 13-4). Fasten part D with hinges to fixed lid section (part G). Part D might need extra sanding and fitting so it moves easily. Center the top (part A) over the finished base assembly. Mark inside of part A where part H should be fastened. Allow at least $3/8$ of an inch between outside top of part B and inside of part H, so the top can move freely up and down (Fig. 13-4). Fasten supports (part H) to bottom of top (part A). Countersink screws and plug with wooden plugs. Make four hinge pins (Fig. 13-6). If you do not have a lathe, make the pins of doweling with wooden knobs glued on for handles. Round the end of the hinge pins with a rasp or sandpaper. Mark location for the hinge pin holes on supports (part H) by marking through holes on top of the sides (parts B). Cut holes in the supports (part H). Put hinge pins in place. Your table is ready to stain or paint as you desire.

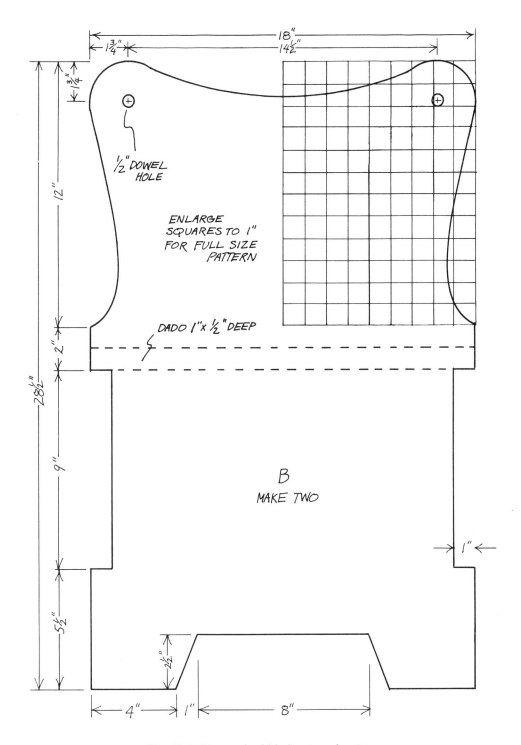

18"

14½"

1¾"

¾"

½" DOWEL HOLE

ENLARGE SQUARES TO 1" FOR FULL SIZE PATTERN

12"

DADO 1" x ½" DEEP

2"

28½"

B
MAKE TWO

1"

9"

5½"

2½"

4"

1"

8"

Fig. 13-3. Plan and gridded pattern for sides.

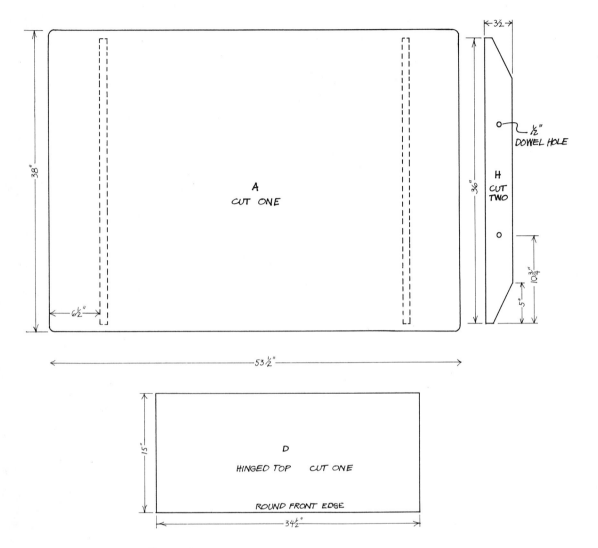

Fig. 13-4. Plan for table top, braces, and hinged top of box.

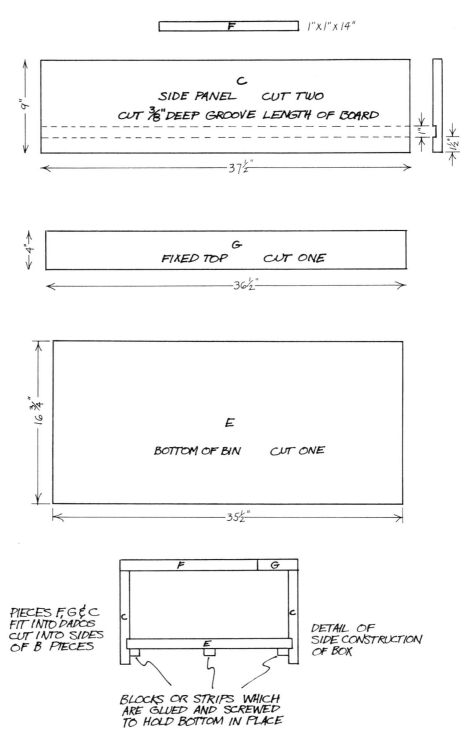

F   1"x 1" x 14"

C
SIDE PANEL   CUT TWO
CUT ⅜" DEEP GROOVE LENGTH OF BOARD

9"

37½"

1"

½"

G
FIXED TOP   CUT ONE

4"

36½"

E

BOTTOM OF BIN   CUT ONE

16 ¾"

35½"

F   G

C   C

E

PIECES F, G & C
FIT INTO DADOS
CUT INTO SIDES
OF B PIECES

DETAIL OF
SIDE CONSTRUCTION
OF BOX

BLOCKS OR STRIPS WHICH
ARE GLUED AND SCREWED
TO HOLD BOTTOM IN PLACE

Fig. 13-5. Plans and assembly for box.

HINGE PIN
MAKE 4

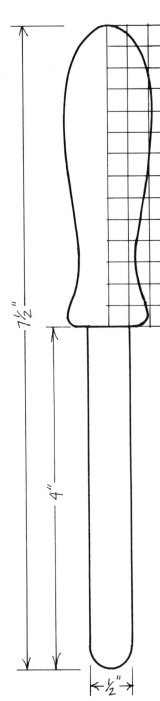

Fig. 13-6. Gridded pattern for hinge pin.

7½"

4"

½"

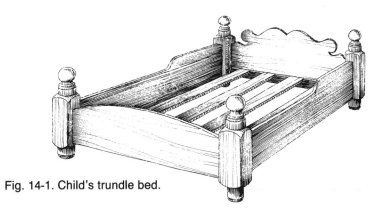

Fig. 14-1. Child's trundle bed.

Trundle Bed

This little trundle bed is a copy of an eighteenth-century Pennsylvania bed. I saw it displayed under an elegant early four-poster in the William Penn Museum in Harrisburg. Usually plain in design, trundles were seldom as handsome as this one is, with its turned posts and scrolled headboard (Fig. 14-1). The bed is fastened together with mortises, dowels, and glue, as was the custom of that period. Nails were in short supply in early America because they were tediously made by hand of metal, which was expensive. I have found that the old mortise-and-dowel joints often hold far better than our screws and nails, which can work out of the wood and tear it as they come out. Perhaps this accounts for so many pieces of old furniture remaining in usable condition today.

These small beds were stored under high full-sized beds where older children and adults slept. In the evening, the trundle bed was pulled out, and the children were put to bed for the night. When morning came, the trundle was pushed back under the big bed to make room for the day's activities. In early homes, where space was at a premium, each room usually had several functions, and the space-saving feature of the trundle bed was certainly an advantage.

Although short enough to slide under most high early beds, this trundle is attractive enough to warrant a room of its own (Fig. 14-2). This design is suitable for a child two to six years old. A standard crib mattress will fit it nicely, with room to tuck in blankets or a quilt. If it is to be used in the traditional way, the large bed's side rails must clear the floor by a least eighteen inches. This bed makes a fine transition between crib and full-sized bed. It can be made longer by extending the slats and side rails. By adding cross supports or a plywood sheet over the slats, the bed can be made extra strong for the active youngsters of today.

This bed is unusual in that it has slats instead of woven rope, and the slats run from headboard to footboard. It is important to make the slats of firm but flexible hardwood so they will be strong enough to support a child who is active.

The original finish on this bed was a barn-red paint that was probably milk-based. I used a good soft-finish acrylic paint, but it could be stained or painted any of the usual colonial colors such as mustard or a greyed blue or green.

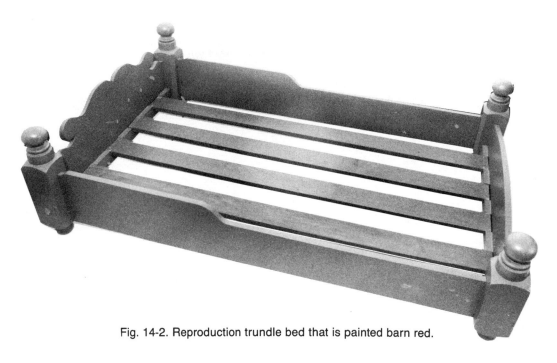

Fig. 14-2. Reproduction trundle bed that is painted barn red.

MATERIALS

Wood:

- 4 pieces, $4 \times 4 \times 16^5/8$ inches clear hardwood for posts
- 1 piece, $^3/4 \times 11^3/4 \times 34$ inches hardwood for headboard
- 1 piece, $^3/4 \times 8 \times 34$ inches hardwood for footboard
- 2 pieces, $^3/4 \times 2 \times 30$ inches hardwood for supports
- 2 pieces, $^3/4 \times 8 \times 56$ inches hardwood for sideboards
- 4 pieces, $^3/4 \times 3^1/2 \times 56$ inch hardwood for slats

- About two feet of $^1/4$-inch hardwood doweling
- Sandpaper and carpenter's glue
- Steel wool
- Paint or stain of your choice

The most difficult part of this project is locating the wood for the posts. It should be clear of any defects, strong, and suitable for turning on a lathe. Because I wanted to paint the bed, I chose poplar, although cherry or maple would have been appropriate for the period when trundles were made and used.

CONSTRUCTION TIPS

If you aren't equipped to do turning yourself, a local woodworking shop will probably be able to do the lathe work for you or you can use the Easy-To-Do plan in Fig. 14-8. Cut full-size templates from the pattern (Figs. 14-3 through 14-7). Trace the pattern into the wood for posts. Trace all four sides and the top (Fig. 14-7). Turn the posts with the aid of templates to check as you turn. Bevel inside edges of posts and cut mortises. Sand the posts well. Trace the patterns for the headboard and footboard sections (Figs. 14-3, 14-4). Cut out headboard and footboard sections and cut tenons in them following the plans. Sand. Cut out slat supports, sand, and fasten to the headboard and footboard (Fig. 14-6). Cut out sideboards. Sand and trim until they fit neatly into mortises on posts (Fig. 14-5). When all parts fit well together, drill holes in posts for dowels, cutting through tenons on headboard and footboard. Cut from outside of posts through post and tenon about 2¹/₄ inches (Figs. 14-9, 14-10). Glue dowels and sideboards in place. Cut slats and sand. Sand and finish entire bed and slats. Put slats in place but do not glue in place (Fig. 14-11).

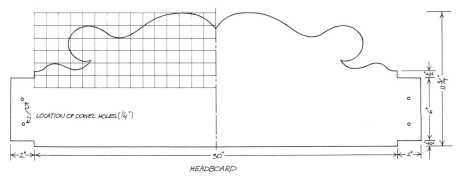

Fig. 14-3. Gridded pattern for headboard.

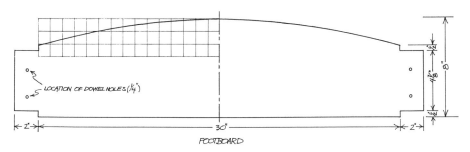

Fig. 14-4. Gridded pattern for footboard.

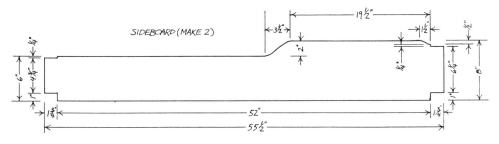

Fig. 14-5. Plan for sideboards.

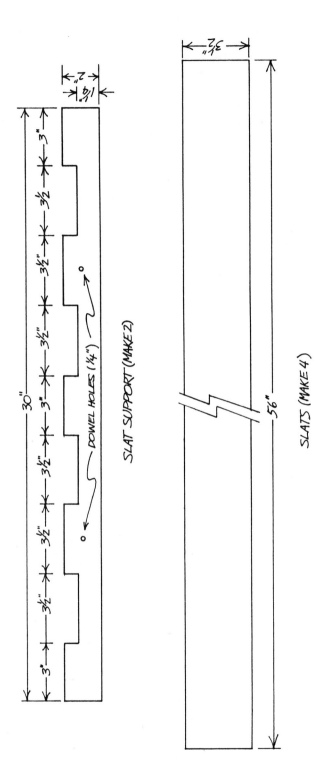

SLAT SUPPORT (MAKE 2)

30"

3" 3½" 3½" 3½" 3" 3½" 3½" 3½" 3"

2"
1½"

DOWEL HOLES (¼")

SLATS (MAKE 4)

3½"

56"

Fig. 14-6. Plan for slat supports and slats.

Fig. 14-7. Gridded pattern for posts.

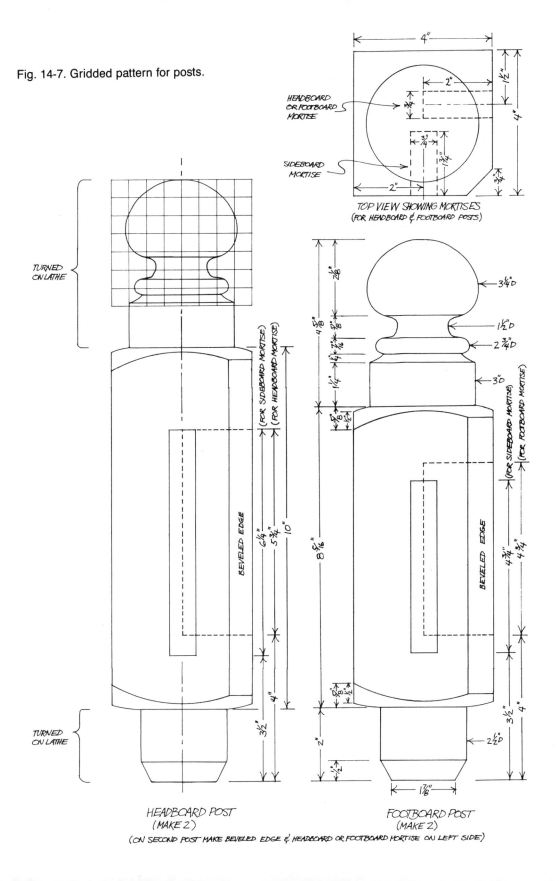

HEADBOARD OR FOOTBOARD MORTISE

SIDEBOARD MORTISE

TOP VIEW SHOWING MORTISES
(FOR HEADBOARD & FOOTBOARD POSTS)

TURNED ON LATHE

(FOR SIDEBOARD MORTISE)
(FOR HEADBOARD MORTISE)

BEVELED EDGE

TURNED ON LATHE

HEADBOARD POST
(MAKE 2)

$3\frac{1}{4}"D$

$1\frac{1}{2}"D$

$2\frac{3}{4}"D$

$3"D$

(FOR SIDEBOARD MORTISE)
(FOR FOOTBOARD MORTISE)

BEVELED EDGE

$2\frac{1}{2}"D$

FOOTBOARD POST
(MAKE 2)

(ON SECOND POST MAKE BEVELED EDGE & HEADBOARD OR FOOTBOARD MORTISE ON LEFT SIDE)

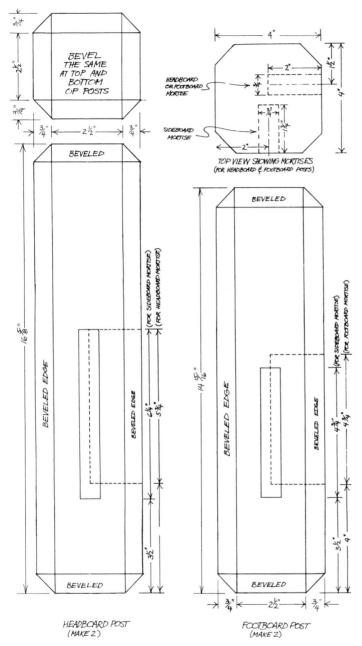

Fig. 14-8. Easy-To-Do plan for posts.

Fig. 14-9. Detail of end post.

Fig. 14-10. Detail of end post from inside bed.

Fig. 14-11. Detail of slats in slat support braces.

PART 3

Toys

Antique toys are rare and expensive. Anyone lucky enough to have a collection of authentic early American toys owns a true and valuable part of Americana. Early settler families had little time or money for toys, and the child with one real doll, toy animal, or any homemade plaything considered himself fortunate. It is indeed surprising that any of the early toys still exist, considering the concentration of love and play given each individual item. The toys we see today are those passed down from one generation to the next and played with by many little hands before coming to rest in museums or private collections.

Some antique toys became traditional in certain regions of the country, and are made in much the same form today as they were long ago. For example, the dancing man or *limberjack* is still made in Appalachia (from the Carolinas north) in the same manner as it was originally. Versions of the woodchoppers are also made in many rural areas today.

Small animals carved of wood or made from skins and homespun were an early favorite of small settlers. Dolls were made by caring mothers using material at hand such as cornhusks and cobs, horns of animals, and bits of leather. Dried apple-head dolls were probably part of the early scene. Animated toys were always special, no matter how jerky the movement. Father's tools and mother's utensils were copied in miniature size for play.

As you make these patterns taken from old toys, be assured the small members of your family will enjoy them as much as the children long ago. A handmade toy has a unique appeal that is missing in the factory-made plastic and metal ones of today.

Fig. 15-1. The woodchoppers, a motion toy.

The Woodchoppers

Simple animated toys like the woodchoppers are typical early American toys. Some feature people chopping, sawing, or hammering, while others depict animals eating, kicking, or fighting. All the motion toys of this genre create movement in the same manner (Figs. 15-1, 15-2, 15-3).

I made my first woodchopper toy while whittling in front of an open fire on a cold winter evening. Undoubtedly, many of the early animated toys were produced by rural men whittling away the long winter evenings in this cheerful occupation.

Make your woodchoppers following my pattern and then let your imagination have free rein, and create your own unique toy.

Fig. 15-2. First position of woodchoppers.

Fig. 15-3. Second position of woodchoppers.

MATERIALS

- Basswood or pine, $1/2 \times 3^{1}/2 \times 12$ inches for two men
- Hardwood, 2 pieces each $1/8 \times 1/2 \times 18$ inches for pulls
- Dowels, $1/8$ inch in diameter, approximately 8 inches long
- One small section of branch (leave bark on) approximately 1 inch in diameter
- Carpenter's glue
- Sandpaper

CONSTRUCTION TIPS

Drill holes for dowels in legs of men before cutting out section between legs (Fig. 15-4). This will help prevent breakage. Be sure holes in pulls are sanded a bit wider in order for the top to move freely when it is worked. Glue dowels in legs if necessary but do not glue to pulls (Fig. 15-5). Men and axes can be shaped and rounded if desired, but be sure to finish men before assembling the toy (Figs. 15-6, 15-7).

Fig. 15-4. View of single woodchopper man, showing how legs fit on supports.

FRONT   SIDE

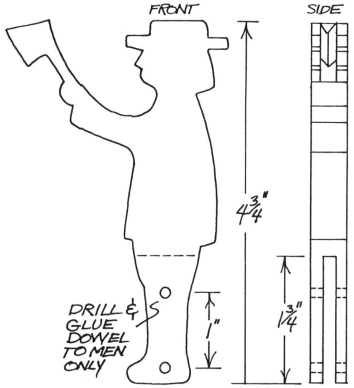

$4\frac{3}{4}"$

$1"$

$1\frac{3}{4}"$

DRILL & GLUE DOWEL TO MEN ONLY

Fig. 15-5. Plan for man.

Fig. 15-6. Full-size pattern for man.

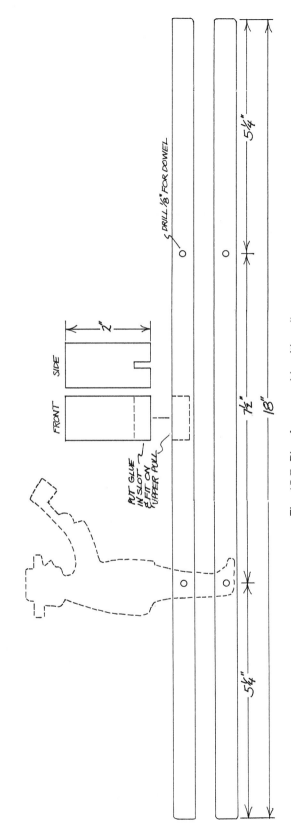

Fig. 15-7. Plan for assembly with pulls.

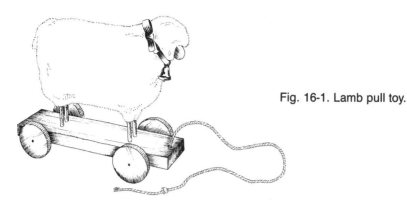

Fig. 16-1. Lamb pull toy.

Lamb Pull Toy

Toy animals have always been a favorite with children. Children of our early settlers treasured animal toys when they were fortunate enough to be given one. When wheels were added to give the animal motion, it was even more desirable.

This lamb pull toy is like many homemade toy animals of its time. It is made with wood and skins with no nails or metal of any kind. Indeed, nails and metal were too rare and expensive in the eighteenth and nineteenth centuries to be used for playthings. The result is a charming toy that is safe for most children to play with and easy to repair, if damaged by too much loving attention (Figs. 16-1, 16-2).

Fig. 16-2. Reproduction lamb pull toy.

My plan stays true in spirit to the original lamb that was worn out from too many loving touches by small hands.

I added a ribbon and a bell to make the lamb more festive. It is a decorative addition under my tree at Christmas and played with much of the year also.

MATERIALS

Pine:

- $1^1/_2 \times 5^1/_4 \times 9$ inches for body of lamb
- $3/_4 \times 2^1/_2 \times 10$ inches for base
- $3/_8 \times 2^1/_4 \times 9$ inches for wheels

$1/_4$-inch dowels:

- 2 pieces $3^1/_2$ inches for front legs
- 2 pieces $2^3/_4$ inches for rear legs
- 2 pieces $3^3/_4$ inches for axles
- Sheepskin or fur fabric to cover body, about a 14-inch square piece
- Red ribbon $1/_4$ inch wide, 6 inches long for neck
- Small bell to hang on ribbon collar
- Carpenter's glue
- Sandpaper
- Flat paint: black, green, and red
- Rough cord for pull, about 24 inches
- Small bead for end of cord

CONSTRUCTION TIPS

Cut body piece from pine and shape the face and neck with sandpaper. Use a knife if necessary (Figs. 16-3, 16-4). Drill holes in body for legs. Cut the base and sand it. Drill holes part way into the base for legs. Drill holes for axles and pull-cord all the way through the base. Cut dowels for legs and axles and sand. (The axles should move freely through the holes). Paint face and underbody of lamb black. Paint base, wheels, axles, and legs. Sand and repaint. When paint is dry, start to cover the body with sheepskin. Drape sheepskin evenly over the body, with open ends at bottom. Leave enough skin at either side to fold around to cover the rear and chest sections. When cutting leather, always cut from

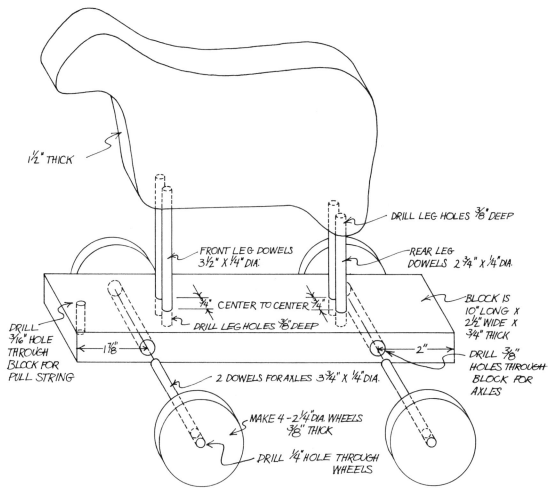

1½" THICK

DRILL LEG HOLES ⅜" DEEP

FRONT LEG DOWELS
3½" X ¼" DIA.

REAR LEG
DOWELS 2¾" X ¼" DIA.

¼" CENTER TO CENTER ¾"

DRILL LEG HOLES ⅜" DEEP

BLOCK IS
10" LONG X
2½" WIDE X
¾" THICK

DRILL
3/16" HOLE
THROUGH
BLOCK FOR
PULL STRING

1⅞

2"

DRILL ⅜"
HOLES THROUGH
BLOCK FOR
AXLES

2 DOWELS FOR AXLES 3¾" X ¼" DIA.

MAKE 4 - 2¼" DIA. WHEELS
⅜" THICK

DRILL ¼" HOLE THROUGH
WHEELS

Fig. 16-3. Exploded plan for lamb.

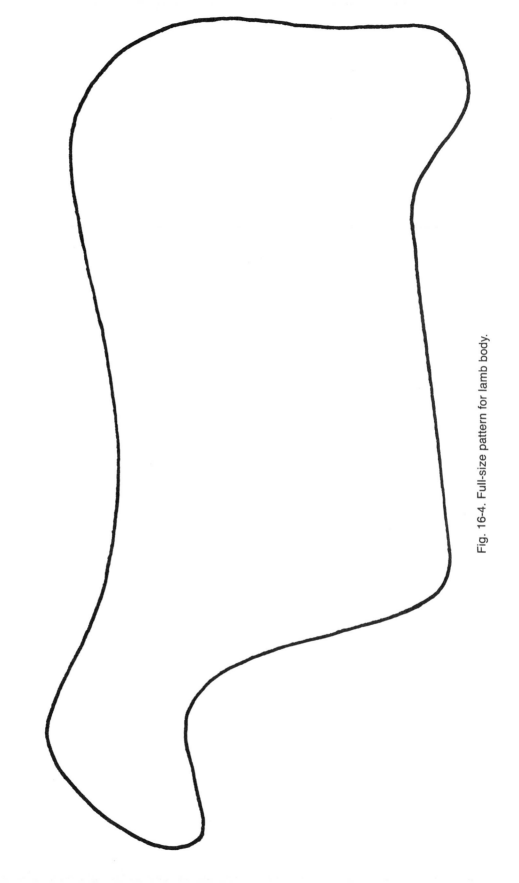

Fig. 16-4. Full-size pattern for lamb body.

wrong side towards right side. Cut at a slant, angling in at wrong side so that the fur on the right side can cover the edge when brushed over the cut. Glue sheepskin to body. Start at top of back, then sides. You will need to stretch the sheepskin to fit and trim as you go (much the same as upholstering furniture). Hold skin in place with a soft cord or rubber bands until glue is dry. NOTE: If you use a synthetic fur, fold fabric, right sides together, and drape over back. Shape and pin fold along spine from head to tail to fit snugly over body. Trim and sew on machine. Turn inside out and proceed as with skin.

Glue skin onto the rear end of the lamb. Pull skin around and trim so each side of skin covers one half of rear, making a middle line. Keep extra skin at top to cut and fold later for a tail. Glue and fasten until dry. When rear section is dry, make the tail. Sheep tails are shaped like a large U. Trim and fold the extra section of skin until a small piece (still attached at top) can be folded and glued down for a proper tail. Fasten in place until dry.

Finish the front of the lamb in much the same way as the rear. Trim the pieces around the chest in the same manner as the rear section, meeting at a center line. Glue and fasten until dry. There will be extra skin over the head section and also hanging down below the body. To finish the head, trim carefully around the black face so that it will show when the skin is glued in place. Glue and fasten until dry. If ears are desired, cut two triangles of sheepskin, about 3/4 inch on each side. Fold and sew with fur on outside, and stitch to the sides of the head. Glue legs in place on the body. Pulling skin around bottom, trim to allow legs through. Glue skin in place. Glue legs into base. Put wheel and axles on the base. Glue wheels to axles. Thread cord through base; knot underneath and put a bead on the pull end. Tie a ribbon and bell around the lamb's neck (Fig. 16-5). Paint eyes and mouth if desired.

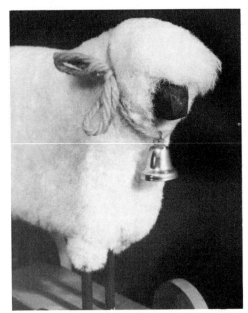

Fig. 16-5. Detail of lamb's face.

Fig. 17-1. Limberjack.

The Limberjack

An old Appalachian toy made entirely of wood, the *limberjack* is a dancing man. His loosely jointed body does a fine clog dance when the "stage" on which his feet rest is tapped in rhythm (Figs. 17-1, 17-2).

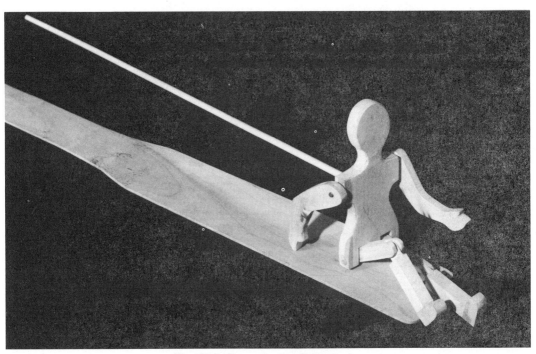

Fig. 17-2. Reproduction limberjack.

These dancing men have been made from very early colonial times throughout the eastern coastal and mountain regions of America. Limberjacks have come to be thought of as an Appalachian toy perhaps because that region has continued its tradition of homecrafts into the present day.

This pattern is typical of the old-time limberjack with its doweled joints and unpainted, simple body. Sometimes the dancing men were shaped more realistically and painted to represent farmers or slaves; sometimes animals such as horses or mules with four dancing legs were depicted. All had much the same construction. The feet should be made of hardwood to make a sharp, precise sound as they dance. It is necessary for the joints to be very loose so the arms and legs will readily swing into motion.

Place the stage on a plank-bottom chair and sit on the rounded end. Holding the limberjack by the dowel in his back so that his feet barely touch the front of the stage, tap the narrowed middle of the stage with the side or fingertips of your other hand. The toy responds to the vibrations and begins to dance in a lively fashion, arms swinging and legs in full motion. By varying the rhythm, you can make the limberjack move his arms and legs alternately, or move his legs alone. You will find that these toys will delight all ages and liven up any gathering.

MATERIALS

Basswood, Pine, or Cherry:

- 1 piece, $1/2 \times 2^{1/4} \times 5^{1/2}$ inches for body
- 2 pieces, $1/2 \times 1/2 \times 5^{1/2}$ inches for legs
- 2 pieces, $1/4 \times 2 \times 3^{1/2}$ inches for arms
- 2 pieces, $1/2 \times 1/2 \times 1$ inch for feet (hardwood)

- 1 $1/16$-inch dowel for joints
- 1 $1/4$-inch dowel for working stick
- 1 $1/8$- $\times 3$- $\times 24$-inch maple or cherry board for stage
- $2^{3/4}$-inch box nails
- Sandpaper and glue for feet

The stage should be about 24 inches long. Shape-in slightly through the middle and round the edge opposite the stage area. Sand carefully to eliminate splinters. Shape stage board as in plan and sand well. Sit on rounded end. The man will dance on the other end.

CONSTRUCTION TIPS

Cut out all pieces, sand carefully, and drill holes as noted on plans (Figs. 17-3, 17-4). Glue feet to lower legs. Fit upper leg parts to body. If holes are drilled carefully, the dowel should fit snugly into body section and loosely through leg section. This enables legs to swing freely. It might be necessary to sand or trim top of legs slightly. When upper legs are working well, trim off dowel close to body on both sides and sand. Proceed by fitting lower legs to upper legs in the same way—the dowels should fit snugly in the holes in the upper legs and loosely through the lower legs. Again, make the necessary adjustments until the legs swing freely. Trim dowels and sand smooth. Nail the arms to the body after drilling holes in the arms. Be careful to drill holes wider than box nails to be used, but smaller than the head of the nails or else the arms will fall off (Fig. 17-5). Put large dowel into hole in back. This is removable to make it easier to move the toy from place to place. Shape the stage board by narrowing through midsection, rounding at end opposite stage, and sanding carefully.

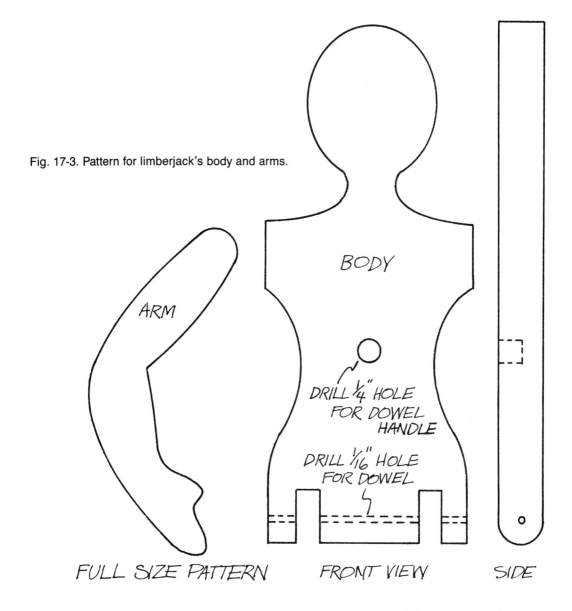

Fig. 17-3. Pattern for limberjack's body and arms.

ARM

BODY

DRILL ¼" HOLE FOR DOWEL HANDLE

DRILL ⅟16" HOLE FOR DOWEL

FULL SIZE PATTERN   FRONT VIEW   SIDE

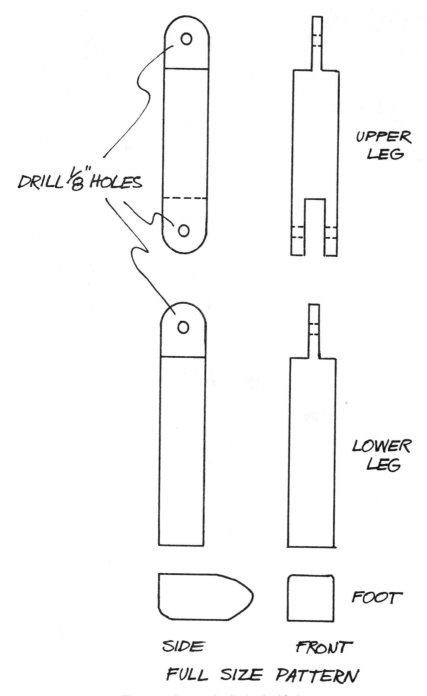

DRILL ⅛" HOLES

UPPER LEG

LOWER LEG

FOOT

SIDE   FRONT

FULL SIZE PATTERN

Fig. 17-4. Pattern for limberjack's legs.

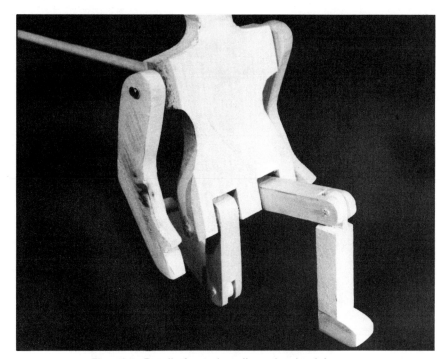

Fig. 17-5. Detail of man kneeling, showing joints.

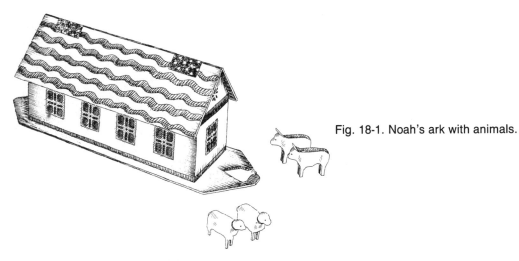

Fig. 18-1. Noah's ark with animals.

Noah's Ark

This Noah's ark is a composite of several early American arks in the William Penn Memorial Museum collection in Harrisburg, Pennsylvania (Figs. 18-1, 18-2). Arks such as this were special Sunday or holiday toys, brought out when more active play was considered inappropriate in the strict religious early households of New England.

Fig. 18-2. Reproduction Noah's ark.

Originally brought to America from middle Europe by early settlers, the arks were later made by local craftsmen, who copied them closely. They incorporated many features such as the flat double-ended base, the scalloped roof that simulates the red tile roofs of Germany, and the colorful stripes that encircle the house section.

Seldom did the arks include any African or exotic animals because most early rural craftsmen had no visual experience with such beasts. Most arks were filled with sets of familiar forest and farm animals. When an occasional early toy maker attempted to depict African animals, the results were often grotesque, fanciful creatures with slight resemblance to their true-life models.

I included farmyard familiars such as horses, goats, sheep, rabbits, deer, cattle, a fox, and a dove. A dove was sometimes glued to the deck of the ark. Shapes of the early animals were often indistinguishable from each other and often of the same size. I have made the shapes a little more realistic while trying to maintain the spirit of the early ark inhabitants.

The animals were painted in common farm colors of yellow ochre, brown, tan, and grey. They were sometimes speckled or spotted and had manes, eyes, and tails. The sheep show the most detail, often having collars of red paint or fabric, and sometimes having rough wool or bits of sheepskin glued to their backs. Entire flocks of sheep were often included rather than a pair, as was usual for the other animals. Some craftsmen whittled the animals in detail, but often they barely shaped silhouettes.

The early arks were very similar in shape, size, and decoration. A basic house shape was glued on a flat double-ended base. The house section had horizontal stripes all around and windows painted on all four sides. The roof was painted yellow ochre with wavy lines of red representing tiles. The roof generally had one side fixed to the house. The other side could be unfastened and lifted up on fabric or leather hinges to reveal the animals inside on a bed of straw. Metal hinges were much too expensive and scarce for early settlers to use on toys.

My ark is a Christmas decoration and is packed away in the studio during the remainder of the year. This year, when I unpacked the ark, I discovered that a mother mouse had cut a little hole in one side and had raised a family in the straw with all the tiny wooden animals.

MATERIALS

The wood for making the sides and roof of the ark and the animals can be found at most hobby or craft stores already sanded on both sides. This saves much time in making this project. I used basswood throughout because it is even-grained, and easy to carve and saw.

Ark:

- 5 pieces of wood, $1/8 \times 4 \times 14$ inches
- 1 piece, $1/4 \times 5 \times 20$ inches
- Carpenter's glue
- Sandpaper—medium, fine, and extra-fine
- Calico, 4×4 inches to make strap hinges
- Paint—flat—white Latex or acrylic flat grey acrylic:
    - white brown
    - black
    - yellow ochre
    - blue
    - vermilion

CONSTRUCTION TIPS

Cut out all pieces of ark and sand. Glue sides and ends together to form main house shape (Figs. 18-4, 18-5). Sand and paint primer coat if needed. Following pattern closely (you can trace it onto ark), paint sides and ends in complete detail. Cut out roof sections and sand. Paint in detail as you did on sides and ends. Cut out base (Fig. 18-3). Sand. Glue house section to base, nailing from under base if necessary. Glue one side of roof to house. Fasten other side of roof first with calico hinges glued to roof sections (Fig. 18-6). Paint ark (Fig. 18-7). Fasten dove to front of base after dove is completed. Fill with straw and add animals when completed.

Animals:

Use four pieces of wood $3/4$-$\times 2^{1}/_2$-$\times 12$-inch wood. Cut basic shape with jig or scroll saw. Finish with X-Acto knife and very fine sandpaper. Glue on antlers and ox horn last (Figs. 18-8 through 18-13).

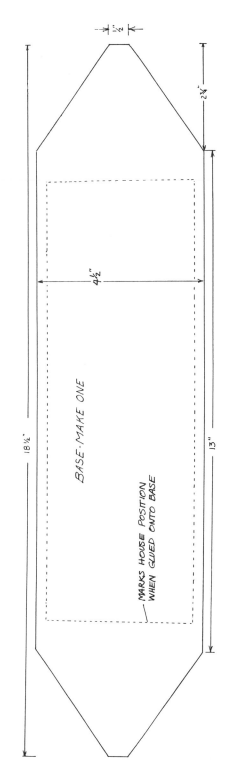

½"

2¼"

4½"

BASE - MAKE ONE

MARKS HOUSE POSITION
WHEN GLUED ONTO BASE

18½"

13"

USE ⅛" BASSWOOD FOR TOP, SIDES AND ENDS
USE ⅜" OR ¼" PLYWOOD OR BASSWOOD FOR BASE

Fig. 18-3. Plan for base.

Noah's Ark   109

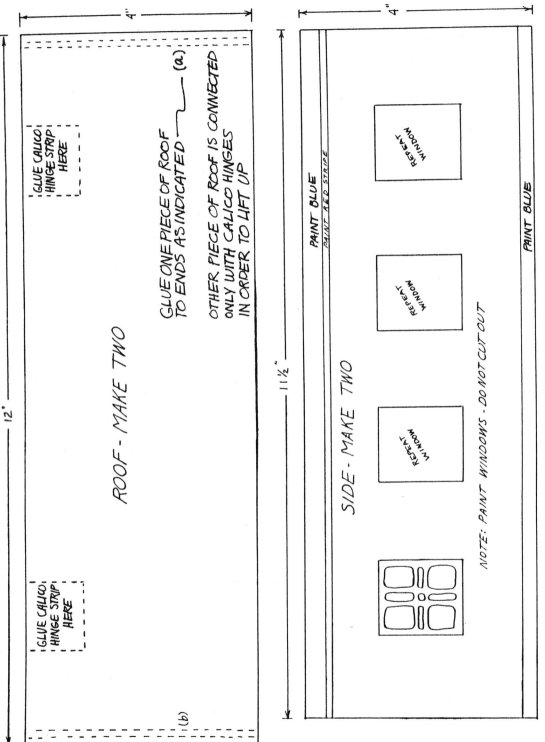

ROOF - MAKE TWO

GLUE CALICO HINGE STRIP HERE

GLUE CALICO HINGE STRIP HERE

GLUE ONE PIECE OF ROOF TO ENDS AS INDICATED — (a)

OTHER PIECE OF ROOF IS CONNECTED ONLY WITH CALICO HINGES IN ORDER TO LIFT UP

12"

4"

(b)

SIDE - MAKE TWO

PAINT BLUE

PAINT RED STRIPE

REPEAT WINDOW

REPEAT WINDOW

REPEAT WINDOW

PAINT BLUE

11½"

4"

NOTE: PAINT WINDOWS - DO NOT CUT OUT

Fig. 18-4. Plan for roof and side pieces, including pattern for painting.

Toy wagon with blocks.
Photograph courtesy of Sterling
Commercial Photography.

Doll furniture with bears.
Photograph courtesy of Sterling
Commercial Photography.

Miniature village made of buildings
typical of 1800.

Noah's ark reproduction.

Reproduction
spoon
rack.

Antique
settle
table.

Reproduction trundle bed
painted barn red as original.

Victorian plant stand filled with flowers. Photograph courtesy of
Sterling Commercial Photography.

Fruit dryer painted blue. Photograph courtesy of Sterling Commercial Photography.

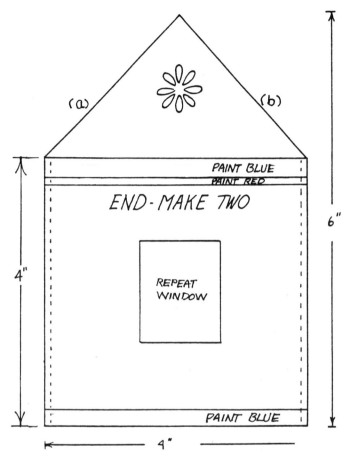

Fig. 18-5. Plan for ends, including pattern for painting.

Fig. 18-6. Detail of roof hinges made of calico.

PAINT DECK GREY

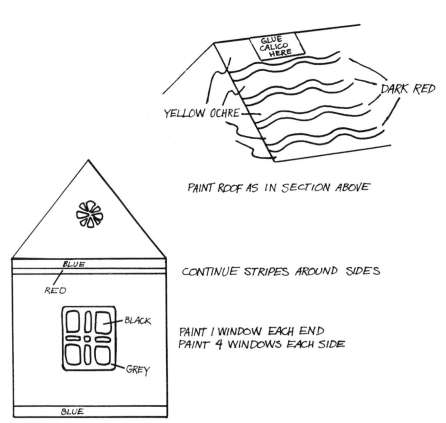

GLUE CALICO HERE

DARK RED

YELLOW OCHRE

PAINT ROOF AS IN SECTION ABOVE

BLUE

RED

BLACK

GREY

BLUE

CONTINUE STRIPES AROUND SIDES

PAINT I WINDOW EACH END
PAINT 4 WINDOWS EACH SIDE

Fig. 18-7. Pattern for painting ark.

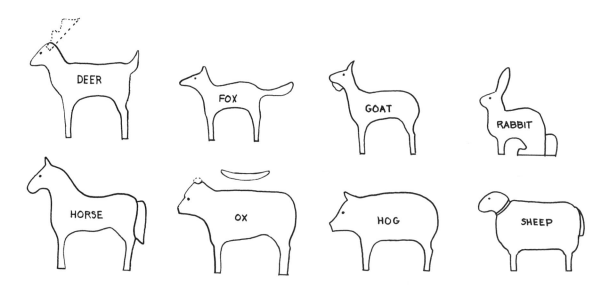

Fig. 18-8. Pattern for antique animals.

Fig. 18-9. Reproduction animals—horse, bull, and pig.

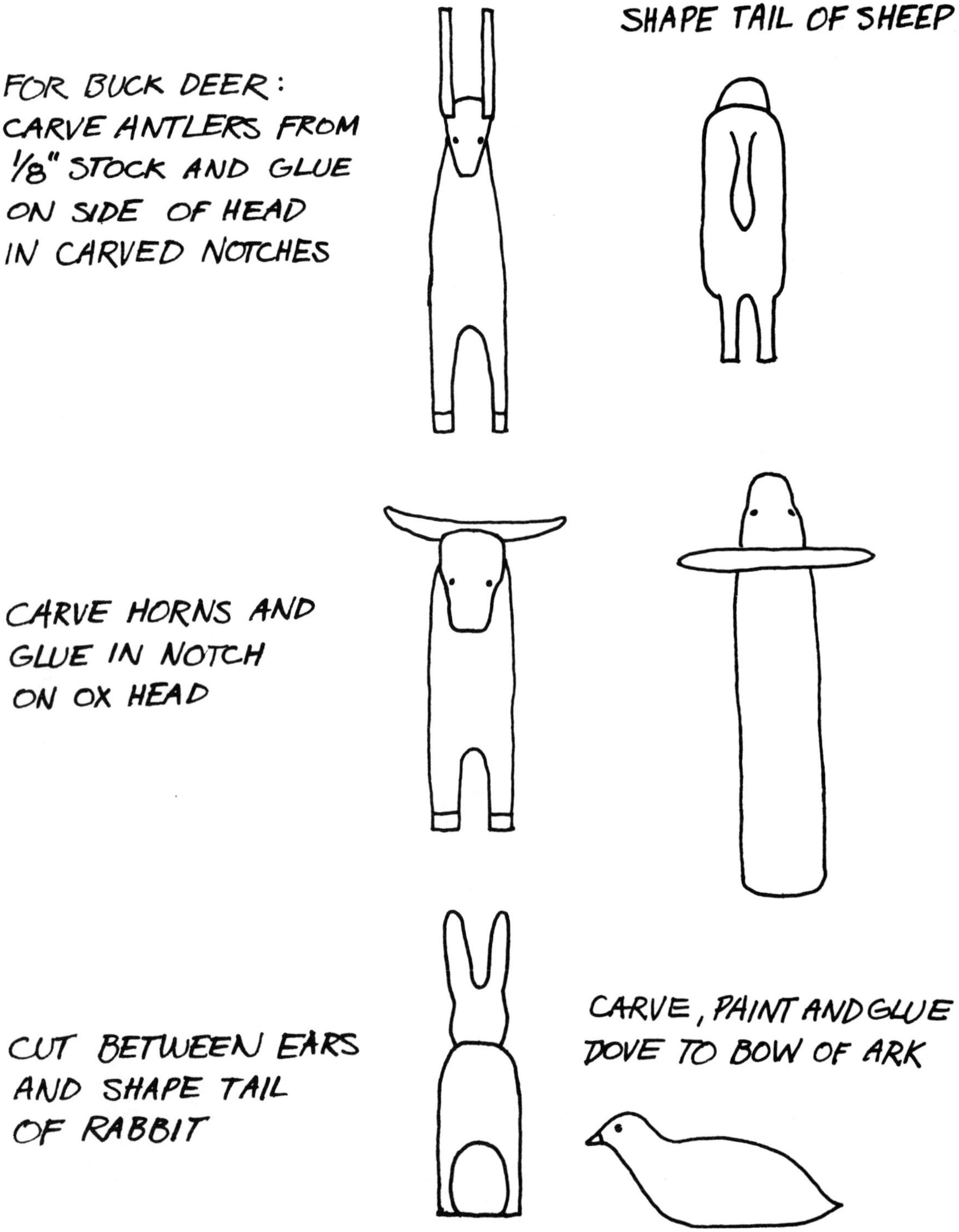

FOR BUCK DEER:
CARVE ANTLERS FROM
1/8" STOCK AND GLUE
ON SIDE OF HEAD
IN CARVED NOTCHES

SHAPE TAIL OF SHEEP

CARVE HORNS AND
GLUE IN NOTCH
ON OX HEAD

CUT BETWEEN EARS
AND SHAPE TAIL
OF RABBIT

CARVE, PAINT AND GLUE
DOVE TO BOW OF ARK

Fig. 18-10. Pattern for animals.

ALL BODIES TAPER AT HEAD - AS TOP VIEW OF OX

TOP BASIC SHAPE

BACK BASIC SHAPE

SHAPE WITH EXACTO KNIFE TO MAKE MORE REALISTIC

CUT BETWEEN LEGS, EARS, INDICATE TAILS, ETC.

SAND WELL WITH EXTRA FINE SANDPAPER BEFORE PAINTING

ANIMALS WERE USUALLY PAINTED IN EARTH COLORS.
SHEEP USUALLY HAD A COLLAR.
SOME ANIMALS WERE SPONGE SPECKLED, SOME DOTTED.
ADD EYES AND TAILS AS DESIRED.

Fig. 18-11. Instructions and plans for animals (1).

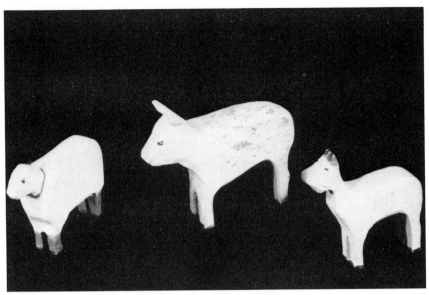

Fig. 18-12. Reproduction animals—sheep, bull, and goat.

Fig. 18-13. Reproduction animals—rabbit, deer, and horse.

Fig. 19-1. Miniature village with houses typical in 1800 America.

Miniature Village

This little village contains buildings typical of those in existence in American colonies in 1800 (Fig. 19-1). You will find a Williamsburg house, a garrison, a salt box house, a small Cape Cod house, a New England farm with the house joined to the barn for ease in doing winter chores, and one-and-a-half story house with eyebrow windows common in New England, and a two-chimneyed inn. These plans also include a covered bridge, an office and a shop, and a church with a steeple.

All of the plans are scaled to match an HO gauge railroad set. The village is a very special accessory to make for use with the old-style train sets.

It's a simple matter to include your own home in the village by adapting the base block plan that most resembles it and adding the details and colors of your own house (Fig. 19-2).

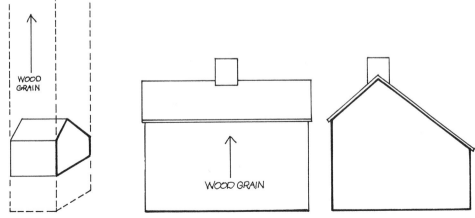

Fig. 19-2. Diagram of how to cut wood for base of houses.

Attention to detail and color gives the village its authentic early American look. Use early colonial paint colors on the outside, and add the details of windows, doors, and shutters very carefully. I used very thin craft wood to cut out the shutters and then glued them onto the base blocks. I also added small signs to the shops.

Easily made with hand tools, this solid little village looks wonderful on a mantle. It is as decorative as it is durable and can be played with by children, making it a delight for the entire family.

At Christmas, I plant the village in cotton-batting snow and add pine trees, small people, and animals. It's a favorite in our home every year. I'm sure you will find the miniature village fun to make and own.

MATERIALS

Basswood or Pine:

- 1 piece, $2^1/_2 \times 4$ inches by 6 feet
- 1 piece, $3 \times 3^1/_2$ inches $\times$ 6 feet
  These are for base blocks; I have allowed for cutting around flaws in the wood.
- 1 piece, $1/_{16} \times 3$ inches by 3 feet for roofing
- 1 piece, $1/_{32} \times 3$ inches $\times$ 3 feet for shutters and signs
- 1 piece, $1/_2 \times 1/_2$ inch $\times$ 2 feet for chimneys
- Carpenter's glue and sandpaper: medium and very fine
- Paint: Latex satin-finish trim paint (interior)
  White primer, flat black, white, pewter grey, grey green, dark olive green, brown, barn red, dark teal blue, yellow ochre, and colonial gold

CONSTRUCTION TIPS

Cut the basic building block using measurements taken from the plans in Figs. 19-2 through 19-16. Sand. Paint with primer. Sand again. Cut roof pieces from $1/_{16}$-inch stock. In most cases the roof overhangs the sides, front, and back of building block—see plans. Sand. Prime paint. Sand. Paint with final color. Glue to basic block. In some cases, you might need to nail with a small brad to secure. Cut chimney from $1/_2$-$\times$-$1/_2$-inch stock. Trim with an X-acto knife and sand to sit firmly on the roof. Paint with primer. Sand lightly. Paint with final color. Glue to the roof. Paint house with final color. Sand very lightly if needed. Paint windows and doors on the building. Cut shutters from $1/_{32}$-inch stock. Sand. Paint with one or two coats as needed. Glue to house. Add details such as hinges, signs, louvers, etc., and touch up.

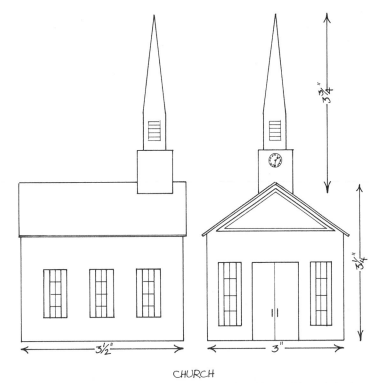

CHURCH

Fig. 19-3. Plan for church based on New Hampshire original.

Fig. 19-4. Note the long, narrow
windows with shutters
and this typical steeple.

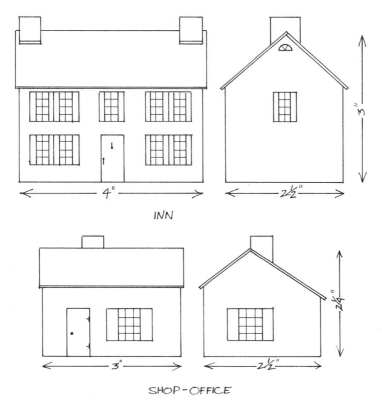

INN

SHOP-OFFICE

Fig. 19-5. Plan for inn and shop based on Massachusetts originals.

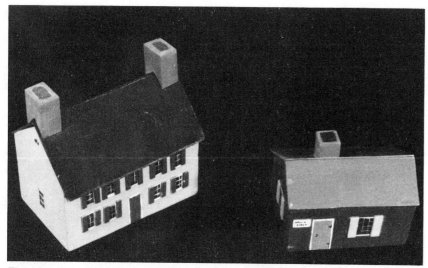

Fig. 19-6. Early large inns were of wood siding, brick, or stone depending on their local materials. Two chimneys were a common feature to heat both sides of the building, which was divided by a central hall. Shops of various kinds were often nearby.

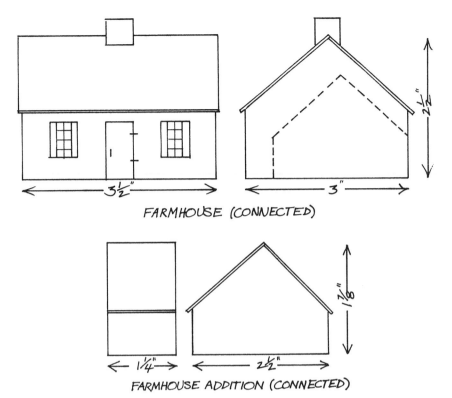

FARMHOUSE (CONNECTED)

FARMHOUSE ADDITION (CONNECTED)

Fig. 19-7. Plan for connected farmhouse and addition based on some found in Maine. Barn (Fig. 19-9) glues onto addition to form three sections in a straight line.

Fig. 19-8. In northern New England, the farmhouses were connected to the barns by use of one or more additions, thus making care of the animals easier in the harsh winter.

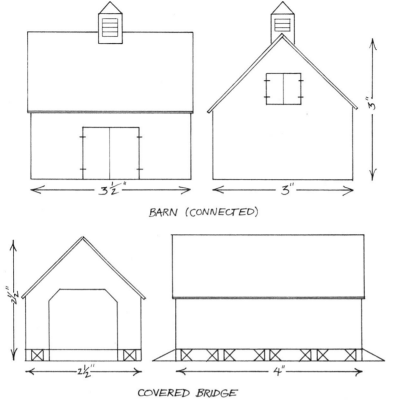

BARN (CONNECTED)

COVERED BRIDGE

Fig. 19-9. Plan for barn from Maine and covered bridge from Pennsylvania.

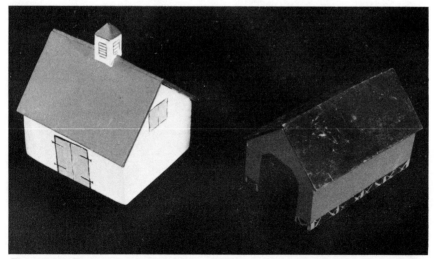

Fig. 19-10. Barn to be connected to addition and covered bridge. Roofs were added to bridges to protect the wooden bridge structure, not to protect people. In winter, snow was shoveled onto the bridge to enable sleighs to pass.

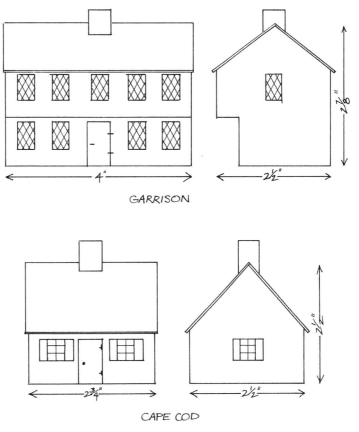

GARRISON

CAPE COD

Fig. 19-11. Plan for Garrison house based on New Jersey home and a cottage from Cape Cod.

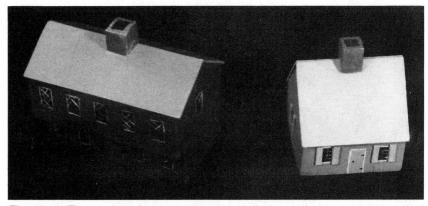

Fig. 19-12. The overhanging second story and diamond window panes are typical of Garrison style similar to those in England at this period. Cape Cods were sided with wooden shakes that weathered to a silver grey. They had few windows, as protection against coastal winds, and high, pitched roofs without dormers.

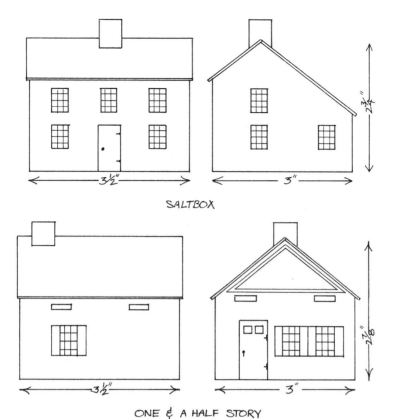

SALTBOX

ONE & A HALF STORY

Fig. 19-13. Plan for saltbox based on a Connecticul original and a one and a half-story (Eyebrow) style from Vermont.

Fig. 19-14. The long sloping roof and lack of exterior shutters were typical of the early saltbox house. It was often painted or stained in a dark red or brown color. The eyebrow house had wide but extremely short windows on the second floor, which was a sleeping loft with low or sloping ceilings.

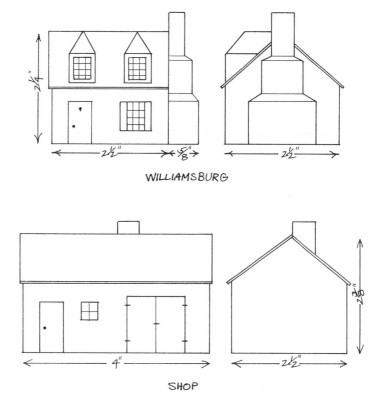

WILLIAMSBURG

SHOP

Fig. 19-15. Plan for Williamsburg cottage and shop based on originals in Virginia.

Fig. 19-16. Typical of the small wooden Virginia homes were the dormer windows, the large exterior brick fireplace structure, and shutters on the windows.

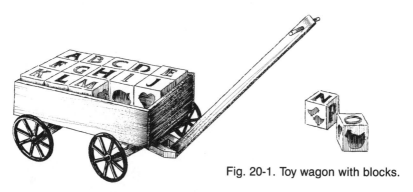

Fig. 20-1. Toy wagon with blocks.

Toy Wagon

Wagons were the main work vehicles in the early settlements of our country. Wagons of all types were used for transporting and hauling in daily life, except when snow covered the ground and sleds were used. Plain, boxlike wagons were the most common, with variations such as the covered wagon with its boatlike sides.

Toy wagons were treasured by little boys who, copying their fathers' work, filled them with blocks or scraps of wood.

This toy wagon is an adaptation of a Victorian one, and is fun to play with or to use for decoration (Figs. 20-1, 20-2). The blocks that fill the wagon have the alphabet and simple animal shapes stenciled on their sides. Make enough blocks to spell out a special child's name or a special message. I have a set that spells "Noel" on one side and "Love" on the other.

If you can't find metal wheels, or want a more rustic, early American look, substitute wooden wheels for the metal ones.

Fig. 20-2. Reproduction wagon loaded with stenciled blocks.

MATERIALS

Blocks: Poplar or clear pine:

- 1 piece, 2 × 2 inches × 3 feet (This will be enough to make about fifteen $1^3/4$-×$1^3/4$-×-$1^3/4$-inch sanded and finished blocks.)

- Sandpaper
- Flat off-white latex paint for base coat
- Stencil mylar (see note)
- Stencil cutter or knife
- Small pointed scissors
- Soft stencil brushes
- Masking tape
- Acrylic craft paint for designs and letters

Note: If you are only making one or two sets, you can substitute contact paper for mylar. This will adhere closely to the blocks without masking tape and give the designs a good clean edge.

Wagon:
Wood:

- 1 piece, $5/16$ × $5^1/2$ × 9 inches for bed
- 1 piece, $5/16$ × $2^3/8$ × $30^1/4$ inches for sides and ends
- 1 piece, $5/8$ × $1^1/2$ × 14 inches for axles
- 1 piece, $3/8$ × 2 × 3 inches for yoke
- 1 piece, $5/8$ × $3/4$ × $11^3/4$ inches for arm

Dowels:

- 1 piece, $3/8$ × $1^9/16$ inches for axle pin
- 1 piece, $3/32$ × $1^1/4$ inches for yoke pin
- 1 piece, $1/4$ × $2^1/2$ inches for arm handle

Miscellaneous:

- Carpenter's glue
- Sandpaper
- Small nails
- Acrylic craft paint for wood
- Four metal wheels about 3 inches in diameter
- Spray metal paint for wheels

CONSTRUCTION TIPS

Wagon

Cut out wagon bed, sides, and ends. Sand well, then glue and nail together (Fig. 20-3). Cut out axles and yoke. Fit yoke to the front axle and glue in place to make yoke assembly (Fig. 20-4). Drill hole for axle pin through wagon bed and into yoke assembly. Do not drill completely through the bottom of the yoke piece. Glue the axle pin to the wagon bed. Drill hole for yoke pin in yoke (Fig. 20-4). Drill tiny hole through the bottom of the yoke to where the axle pin reaches. This hole must be only wide enough for the shaft of a large-headed box nail; this nail will hold the whole assembly up on the axle pin and enable it to move freely without falling off). Tap nail into hole. Cut, drill, and sand arm (Fig. 20-5). Insert handle and mount on yoke. Paint the entire wagon. Paint wheels and let dry completely before attaching to the wagon (Figs. 20-6, 20-7).

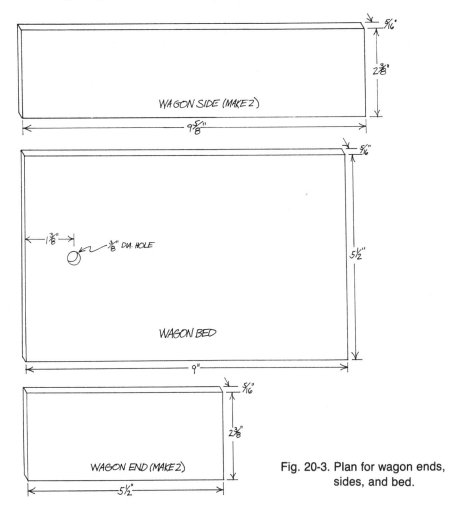

Fig. 20-3. Plan for wagon ends, sides, and bed.

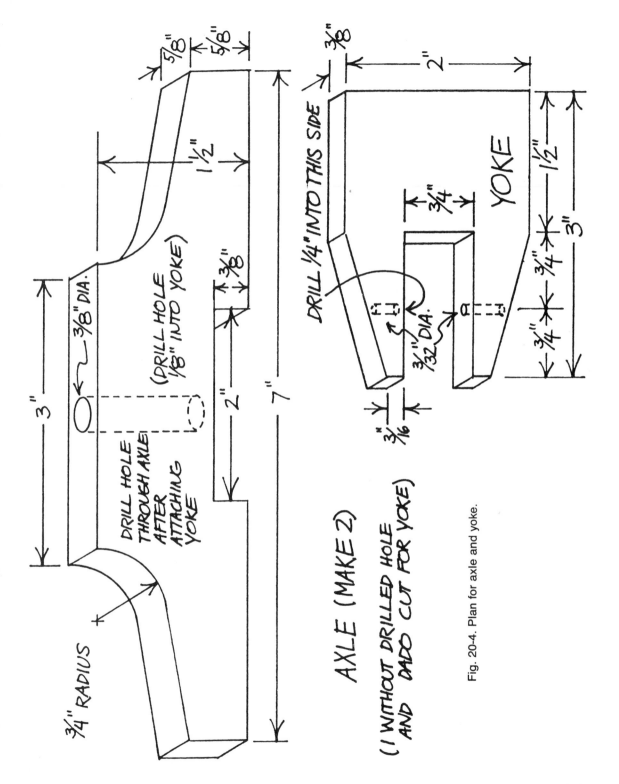

5/8"

1 1/2"

3/8" DIA.

3"

3/4" RADIUS

DRILL HOLE THROUGH AXLE AFTER ATTACHING YOKE

(DRILL HOLE 1/8" INTO YOKE)

3/8"

2"

7"

DRILL 1/4" INTO THIS SIDE

3/8"

2"

3/4"

3/32" DIA.

YOKE

1/2"

3/4"

3"

3/4"

3/16"

AXLE (MAKE 2)

(1 WITHOUT DRILLED HOLE AND DADO CUT FOR YOKE)

Fig. 20-4. Plan for axle and yoke.

Toy Wagon   129

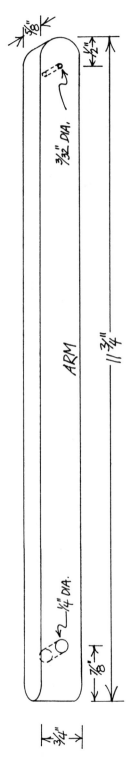

5/8"

3/32" DIA.

ARM

11 3/4"

1/2"

1/4" DIA.

7/8"

3/4"

Fig. 20-5. Plan for handle.

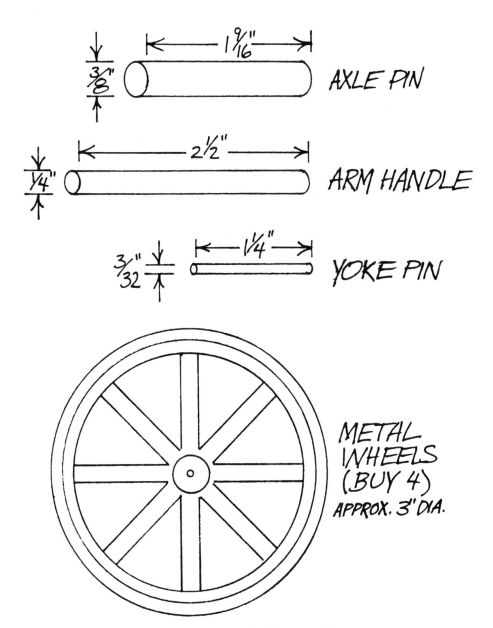

AXLE PIN

ARM HANDLE

YOKE PIN

METAL WHEELS (BUY 4) APPROX. 3" DIA.

Fig. 20-6. Plan for wheels and small parts.

ASSEMBLY

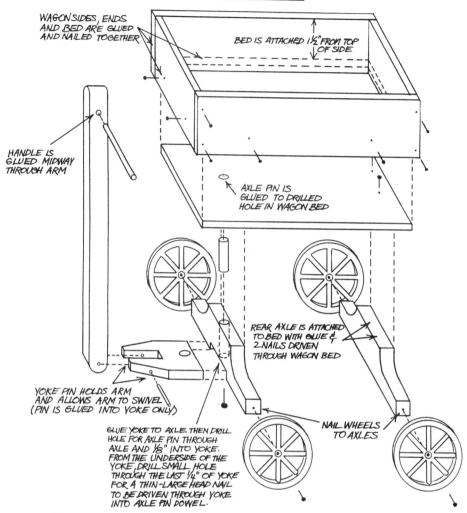

WAGON SIDES, ENDS AND BED ARE GLUED AND NAILED TOGETHER

BED IS ATTACHED 1½" FROM TOP OF SIDE

HANDLE IS GLUED MIDWAY THROUGH ARM

AXLE PIN IS GLUED TO DRILLED HOLE IN WAGON BED

YOKE PIN HOLDS ARM AND ALLOWS ARM TO SWIVEL (PIN IS GLUED INTO YOKE ONLY)

REAR AXLE IS ATTACHED TO BED WITH GLUE & 2 NAILS DRIVEN THROUGH WAGON BED

GLUE YOKE TO AXLE THEN DRILL HOLE FOR AXLE PIN THROUGH AXLE AND ⅛" INTO YOKE. FROM THE UNDERSIDE OF THE YOKE, DRILL SMALL HOLE THROUGH THE LAST ¼" OF YOKE FOR A THIN-LARGE HEAD NAIL TO BE DRIVEN THROUGH YOKE INTO AXLE PIN DOWEL.

NAIL WHEELS TO AXLES

(AXLE/YOKE ASSEMBLY MOVES FREELY WHILE WAGON BED, AXLE PIN AND NAIL ARE STATIONARY)

Fig. 20-7. Exploded view of assembly.

Blocks

Cut out blocks in 1³/₄-inch cubes (Fig. 20-8). Sand well, Paint. Sand again. Paint again. Let dry. There should be 15 blocks. Stencil (see directions) one side of each block with a letter, A through O, using a variety of colors. Turn blocks over and stencil same letter on opposite side. Then turn blocks on sides and, starting with Z on the block already stencilled with As, stencil backwards through the alphabet to P—A,Z; B,Y; C,X; etc. Turn blocks over and stencil same letter on opposite side. You will have four blocks left without a second letter; use these for extra letters of your own choice. Two sides of *each* block will be left to stencil with animals or hearts.

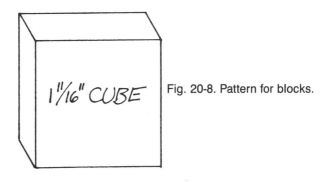

Fig. 20-8. Pattern for blocks.

How to Stencil

Tape or adhere stencil tightly to surface of block (Fig. 20-9). Allow enough outside of the pattern to completely cover surface and to protect it from splatters. Put about a half teaspoon of paint in a dish. Dip tip of stencil brush in paint. Holding brush perpendicular to the surface of a stack of four paper towels, wipe most of the paint off by rubbing in a circular motion. When brush seems almost dry, start to stencil around outside edge by moving brush either up and down or in a circular motion. When the color is as you want it, stop. Remove stencil, and pattern should be complete. If you have made a mistake, repaint with base color and start again. Minor mishaps can be corrected with a small watercolor brush.

Fig. 20-9. Pattern for stenciled letters. Cut from mylar or contact paper.

Fig. 21-1. Ferris wheel.

Ferris Wheel

The great wheel that Gale Ferris designed for the World's Columbian Exposition, held in Chicago in 1893, caught the imagination of a public already intrigued with engineering feats. The Ferris wheel quickly became a standard attraction at carnivals and country fairs, and inspired the original of this charming folk toy (Figs. 21-1, 21-2).

Fig. 21-2. Reproduction Ferris wheel.

This adaptation is painted in bright colors instead of the grey used on the nineteenth-century one, and it can be made with simple hand tools. It is assembled without nails. The doweling used might eventually bend a little out of shape, but by adjusting the hanging wires from time to time you can make sure the wheel rotates in quite satisfactory circles, to give rides to small dolls, or just to serve as an amusing decoration.

MATERIALS

Pine (unless otherwise indicated):

- 2 pieces, $3/4 \times 15/16 \times 17^7/8$ inches for uprights
- 2 pieces, $1 \times 1^1/4 \times 8^1/4$ inches for bases
- 2 pieces, $1/4 \times 3/4 \times 7^7/8$ inches for braces
- 1 piece, $5/8 \times 5/8 \times 5$ inches for axle
- 4 pieces, $5/16 \times 3/8 \times 4^1/2$ inches for crossbars
- 61 inches of $1/4$-inch doweling
- $2 \times 2^1/8 \times 22$ inches of balsa or basswood to make gondola cars
- $1/16 \times 2^1/8 \times 44$ inches of basswood or lightweight, strong wood for gondola car sides
- 84 inches of wire heavy enough to hold shape but easy to bend by hand
- Glue, sandpaper, and paint
  (I prefer using only glue in construction, but you can use small brads if you desire to strengthen the joints).

CONSTRUCTION TIPS

Assemble Stand

Cut out all pieces, sand, and glue together. Be sure to glue one pivot dowel in place, but leave the other out until you mount the wheel in place. Paint as desired (Figs. 21-3, 21-4).

Assemble Wheel

Cut out and drill all sections. Glue dowels into axle at center of axle. Glue cross bars onto ends of dowels (Fig. 21-5). Sand and paint. Mount wheel in place on pivot dowels. Some sanding and fitting might be necessary before wheel will rotate freely. Glue second dowel in place.

Assemble Gondola Cars

Cut out bases, sand. Cut out sides, sand and glue to bases (Fig. 21-6). Drill holes for wire supports. Paint as desired.

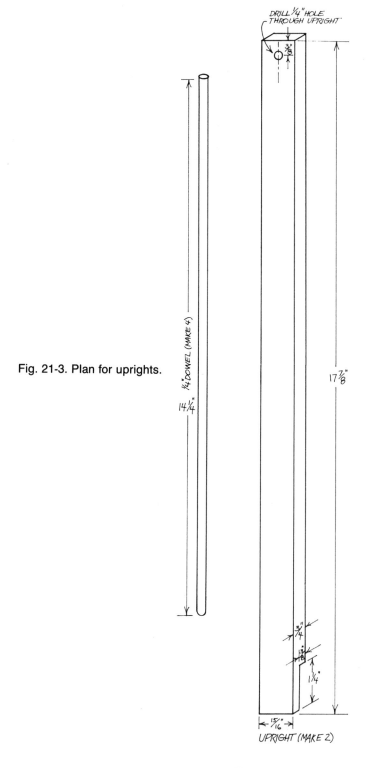

Fig. 21-3. Plan for uprights.

DRILL ¼" HOLE
THROUGH UPRIGHT

⅜"

17⅞"

¼" DOWEL (MAKE 4)

14¼"

¾"

⅛"

1¼"

¹⁵⁄₁₆"

UPRIGHT (MAKE 2)

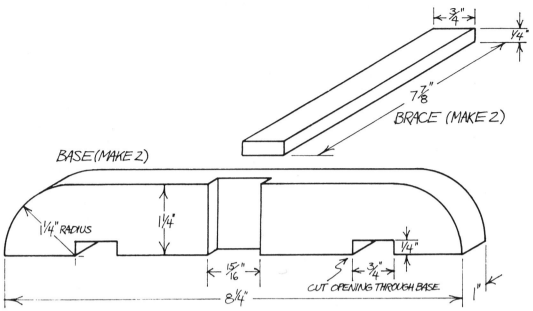

Fig. 21-4. Plan for base and brace.

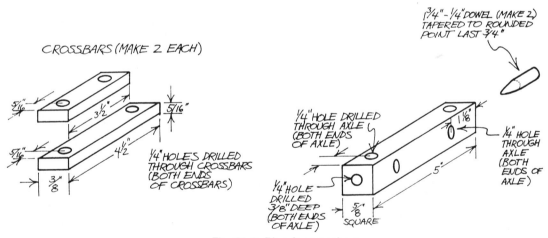

Fig. 21-5. Plan for crossbars.

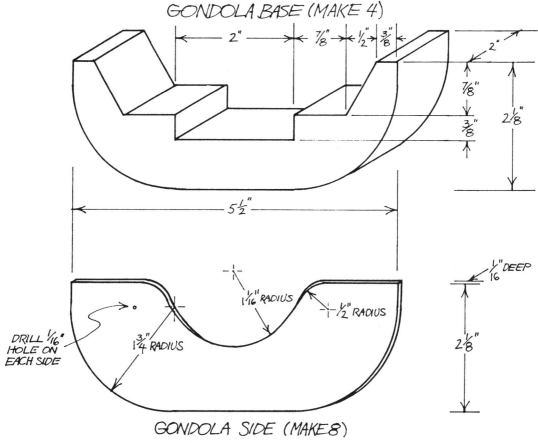

Fig. 21-6. Plan for gondola cars.

Hang Gondola Cars

Bend ends of wire $1/4$ inch as shown (1) in Fig. 21-7. Bend wires in half with center looping around cross bars (2). Cross wires under the cross bars (3), and insert bent ends into sides of cars. Crimp ends upward to hold. After all cars are hung, adjustments can be made by bending wires to allow cars to hang level and rotate freely when wheel is turned.

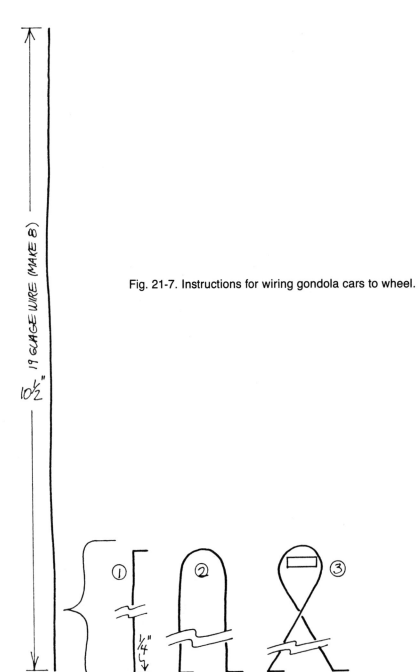

Fig. 21-7. Instructions for wiring gondola cars to wheel.

PART 4

Doll Furniture

Handmade doll furniture is one of the earliest of all toys. Used throughout the centuries to amuse a child while teaching her basic homemaking skills, doll furniture reflects the adult living style of the country and period when it was fashioned.

Doll furniture appeared early in colonial America. Little girls with only rag or cornhusk dolls enjoyed small wooden beds, chairs, or cradles made by fathers and brothers from scraps around the homestead. Well-worn early doll furniture commands high prices in shops and auctions today, and unless you have a priceless early antique doll who demands the authentic antique, it is better to make reproductions using these patterns.

Early cabinetmakers sometimes had shops of their own, but often they travelled from settlement to settlement making furniture to custom order. They had notebooks with sketches of furniture, and often arrived with exact miniatures so the customer could examine the workmanship before ordering. These charming small bureaus, chairs, beds, etc. are often mislabeled as doll furniture. They do make exquisite doll furniture, but their original purpose was strictly commercial. Actual doll furniture of the settlers and up into the present day is always a much-simplified form of the full-sized prototype.

My patterns for the rope bed, cradle, sled, and chair are scaled for the average 10-to 13-inch doll. By enlarging or reducing the patterns you can make them fit any doll or dollhouse.

I have crafted the chairs in all sizes and often in sets of three sizes for three bears.

All of these pieces of doll furniture can be made in this scale—one inch equals one foot for doll houses. When making chairs in this scale, I used round toothpicks for chair rungs and string for the seats.

These toys can be made for child's play or for holiday decorations. They are all easily made with hand tools or a whittling knife, and are a great project for beginning woodworkers.

Fig. 22-1. Doll chair.

Chair

This little ladder back chair can be made in any size to fit your favorite doll. Dollhouse size can be made in basswood or any easy-to-work wood without regard for strength, but if you make a large chair that a child can try to sit on, be sure to use good, strong wood throughout (Figs. 22-1, 22-2, 22-3).

Part of the fun of making this chair is weaving its little seat. If you have never woven a seat, it will prove to be a useful new skill. I have revived many porch rockers and other auction chairs and stools by weaving rush and cord in this manner. I like to spray full-size seats with a protective varnish.

Whatever size chair you make, be sure to paint or refinish the wood before you proceed to make the seat.

Fig. 22-2. Doll chair.

Fig. 22-3. Doll chairs in two sizes. Notice proportions are slightly different as these were custom-made to fit specific dolls.

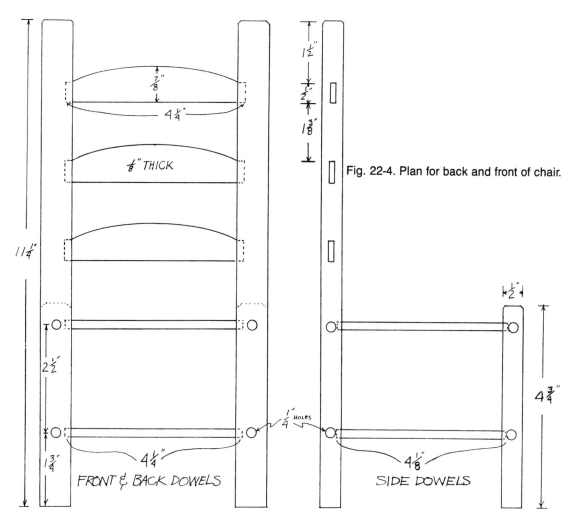

Fig. 22-4. Plan for back and front of chair.

$\frac{7}{8}''$

$4\frac{1}{4}''$

$\frac{1}{8}''$ THICK

$1\frac{1}{2}''$

$\frac{1}{2}''$

$1\frac{3}{8}''$

$\frac{1}{2}''$

$4\frac{3}{4}''$

$11\frac{1}{4}''$

$2\frac{1}{2}''$

$\frac{1}{4}''$ HOLES

$1\frac{3}{4}''$

$4\frac{1}{4}''$

FRONT & BACK DOWELS

$4\frac{1}{8}''$

SIDE DOWELS

MATERIALS
Pine or clear hardwood:
- 1 piece, $1/2 \times 3/4 \times 32$ inches for legs
- 1 piece, $1/8 \times 7/8 \times 12^3/4$ for ladders
- 1 piece, $1/4$-inch dowel 36 inches long
- Rough brown twine for rush seat
- Carpenter's glue
- Paint, stain, and varnish

Note: This chair can be made larger or smaller to fit your needs by lengthening legs and dowels in proportion to each other.

CONSTRUCTION TIPS

Cut pieces as specified in Fig. 22-4. Chair ladders should taper from $7/8$ inch at center to $1/2$-inch tabs about $1/4$ inch long at each end. Chisel, or drill and chisel slots for the ladders in the legs. Drill $1/4$-inch diameter holes about $1/8$-inch deep for dowels to make the seat frame and lower support frame. Assemble chair before gluing to make certain all fits well. Sand or wedge wood chips as needed for a tight fit. Glue and hold together with clamps or rubber bands until dry. Paint, stain, and varnish before rushing seat. Fasten twine on rear dowel as in sketch and proceed around until complete, working all loose ends into rushing so they do not show from either side (Fig. 22-5). Tie end when finished and weave loose ends into rushing. Varnish seat if desired.

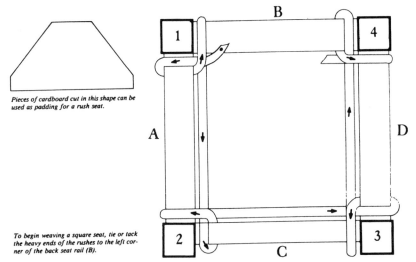

Pieces of cardboard cut in this shape can be used as padding for a rush seat.

To begin weaving a square seat, tie or tack the heavy ends of the rushes to the left corner of the back seat rail (B).

Fig. 22-5. This diagram shows how the seat is woven. Tack cord or rush to back top rung at corner of A and B. Go over and around A, over and around B, and pull toward front of chair. Go over and around front rung C, over and around A at corner #2. Then pull toward side D, and go over and around D at corner #3. Go over and around C and pull toward back B. Go over and around B at corner #4. Go over and around rung D and pull toward A. Repeat in same direction and manner until seat is completely filled in. Fasten end of cord by weaving into underside of seat.

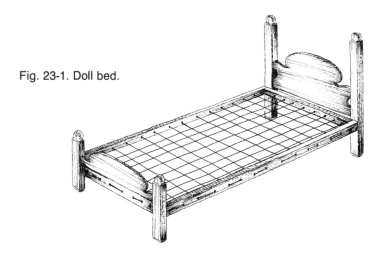

Fig. 23-1. Doll bed.

Bed

Rope beds were very common in early homes. They were easy to take apart to move from place to place and up narrow staircases to sleeping lofts. When disassembled, the parts were merely tied together like a bunch of lumber and moved from place to place as easily as their owner. Fitted together and strung, they were rather like hammocks on legs, and when completed with a feather mattress or straw sack, they made a comfortable resting place (Figs. 23-1, 23-2, 23-3).

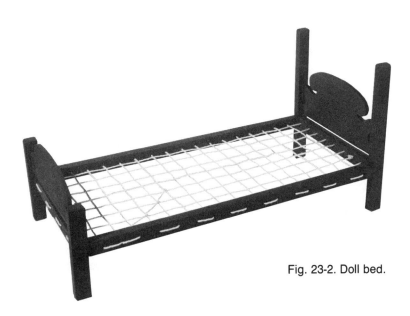

Fig. 23-2. Doll bed.

Fig. 23-3. Doll with undressed bed.

When you look at antique beds, be sure to check for rope knobs along the sides. If there are none, you can sometimes feel where they have been removed. Our family has several old rope beds, but they were long ago altered to hold springs. Some still have the original knobs, while others were cut away. Part of the fun of looking at antiques is discovering how they have been changed by various owners over the years.

MATERIALS

Pine or Hardwood:

- 1 piece, $1/2 \times 3/4 \times 82$ inches for rails and posts
- 1 piece, $1/8 \times 3^{1}/4 \times 8$ inches for headboard
- 1 piece, $1/8 \times 1^{7}/8 \times 8$ inches for footboard

- Ball of white cord for roping
- Small nails and carpenter's glue
- Paint and varnish

CONSTRUCTION TIPS

Cut pieces according to pattern (Fig. 23-4). Drill $1/4$-inch holes all the way through the rails. Cut a flange or foot $1/2$ inch long, $3/8$ inch high, from the bottom of both ends of the headrail and footrail. Cut a flange or foot $1/2$ inch long, $3/8$ inch high, from top of both ends of siderails. Fit the siderails to the headrail and footrail (Figs. 23-5, 23-6). Cut out a piece of the post $1/2 \times 3/4 \times 1/2$ inch to fit the rail flanges into (Fig. 23-4). Chisel, or drill and chisel pockets in the posts for the headboard and footboard flanges (Fig. 23-4). Make the openings smaller rather than larger for a tight fit and a secure piece of furniture. Sand the flanges or wedge in pieces of wood to make the joints snug. Assemble bed before gluing. Take apart, glue, nail, and clamp until dry. Paint or stain, and varnish. Rope bed: To cut cord, multiply length of long rail, plus 2 inches, times the number of holes in the short rail for roping parallel to the long rail; multiply the length of the short rail, plus 2 inches, times the number of holes in the long rail for roping parallel to the short rail. Start at the rear of the head rail, knotting cord to fasten. Proceed threading cord as in Fig. 23-7 until roping in one section is finished. Start with the other section in the same manner but at the hole near the headboard on the long rail. Note: 1) Bed can be lengthened or shortened by adjusting length of long rails by one inch increments. 2) Be sure to include flanges when cutting out headboard and footboard.

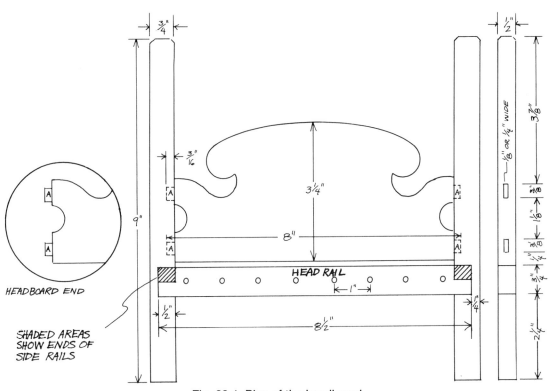

Fig. 23-4. Plan of the headboard.

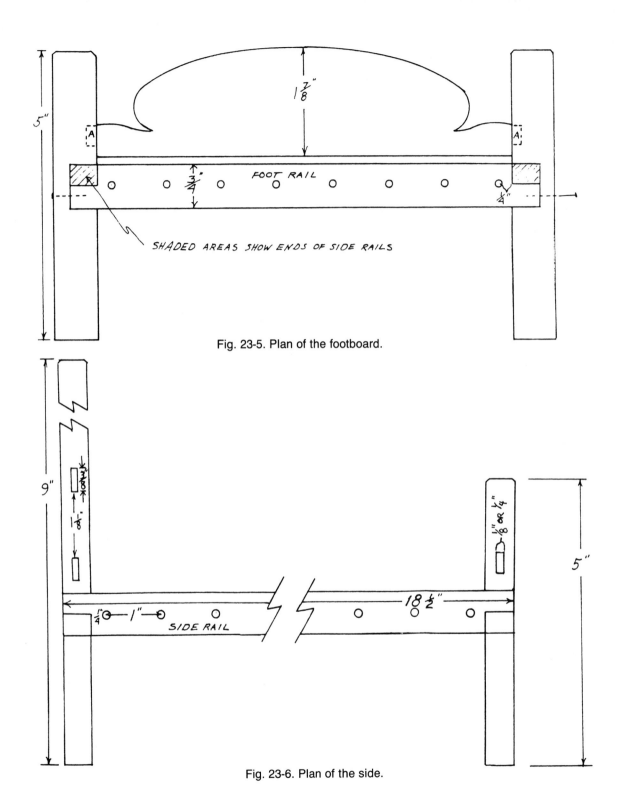

Fig. 23-5. Plan of the footboard.

Fig. 23-6. Plan of the side.

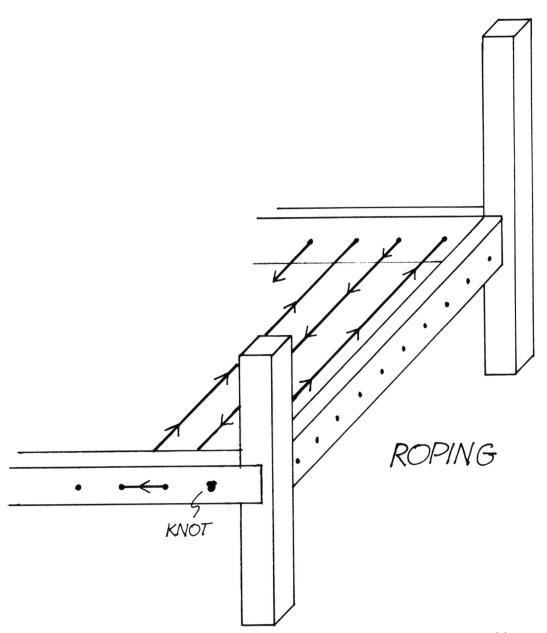

KNOT

ROPING

Fig. 23-7. Method of roping the bed after it is completely finished, with either paint or varnish.

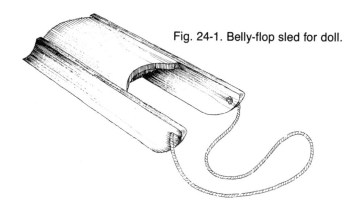

Fig. 24-1. Belly-flop sled for doll.

Sled

Sleds were important work implements, rather than toys, on early farms. From New England and westward, wherever snow covered the ground for portions of the year, sleds were used for transporting and hauling. Many heavy jobs were scheduled for the snowy times when sleds could easily traverse rough terrain that would have been impossible for wagons to cross. Easy to construct and easy to load, sleds were often the only vehicle of the early homesteader.

The low, sturdy sled pulled by oxen, horses, or even people was used by early settlers as they moved westward. Those who could afford the luxury of two sleds often had a more delicate sleigh for the family to ride in.

Some sleds were made for boys and girls to play with and to pull the toddlers when the snow was deep. The early sleds had wooden runners that were waxed to create a more slippery surface. Later, a major improvement in mobility and durability was the addition of metal strips to the runners.

You can make two different sleds from my pattern. The one with sides and back was copied after a sled used to pull small children or invalids; the other is a version of the older child's belly-flop style (Figs. 24-1, 24-2, 24-3).

These little sleds make charming Christmas decorations and gifts. Tie a box of goodies on top, decorate with holly and a bow and use as a centerpiece or give to a friend.

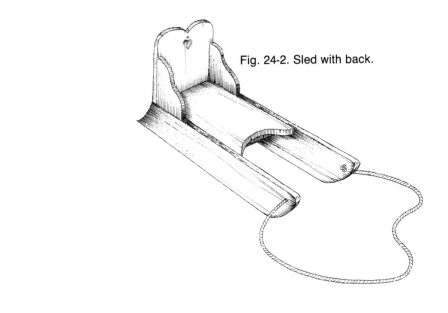

Fig. 24-2. Sled with back.

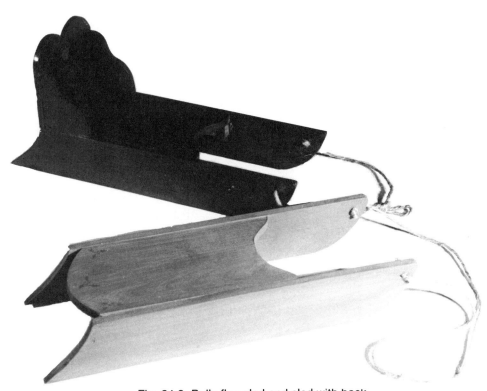

Fig. 24-3. Belly-flop sled and sled with back.

MATERIALS

Pine:

- 1 piece, $1/4 \times 2^1/4 \times 30$ inches for runners
- 1 piece, $1/4 \times 4^1/8 \times 7^3/4$ inches for seat
- 1 piece, $1/2 \times 3/4 \times 19^1/2$ inches for undersupports
- 1 piece, $1/4 \times 4^5/8 \times 4$ inches for back of large sled
- 1 piece, $1/4 \times 2^7/8 \times 5$ inches for two sides of large sled

- Carpenter's glue and nails
- Paint and varnish
- Rough brown twine for rope

CONSTRUCTION TIPS

Cut support pieces. Glue and nail together as shown in Figs. 24-4 and 24-5. Cut and drill the holes in the runners (Fig. 24-6). Glue and nail the runners to the long sides of the support frame leaving $1/4$ inch above the frame. Glue and/or nail seat on support frame. Seat should be flush with runners. Sand if needed. For large sled, glue or nail the back, then sides (Fig. 24-7). Paint. When dry, decorate. Varnish. Tie twine through holes in runners.

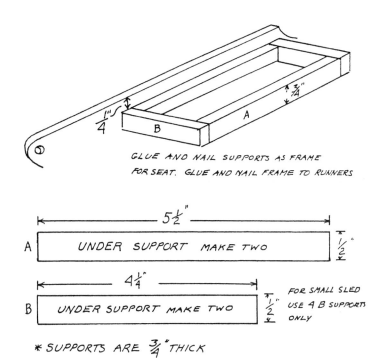

GLUE AND NAIL SUPPORTS AS FRAME

FOR SEAT. GLUE AND NAIL FRAME TO RUNNERS

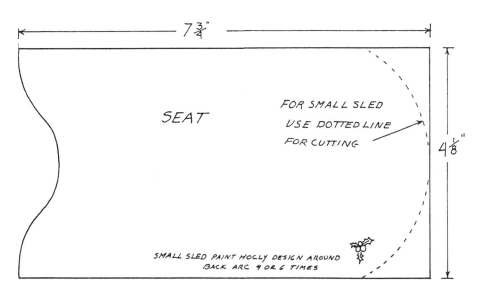

A | UNDER SUPPORT MAKE TWO $5\frac{1}{2}"$ $\frac{1}{2}"$

B | UNDER SUPPORT MAKE TWO $4\frac{1}{4}"$ $\frac{1}{2}"$

FOR SMALL SLED
USE 4 B SUPPORTS
ONLY

* SUPPORTS ARE $\frac{3}{4}"$ THICK

$7\frac{3}{4}"$

SEAT

FOR SMALL SLED
USE DOTTED LINE
FOR CUTTING

$4\frac{1}{8}"$

SMALL SLED PAINT HOLLY DESIGN AROUND
BACK ARC 4 OR 6 TIMES

ALL WOOD IS $\frac{1}{4}"$ THICK

EXCEPT SUPPORTS

Fig. 24-4. Plan for sled base for both styles of sled.

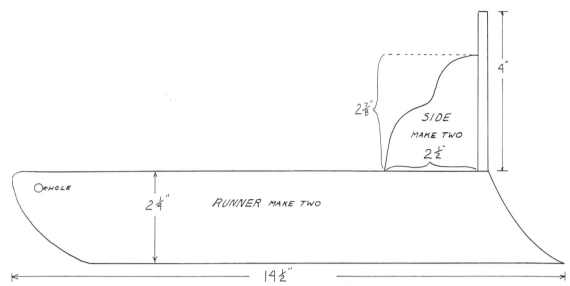

4"

$2\frac{7}{8}$"

SIDE

MAKE TWO

$2\frac{1}{2}$"

HOLE

$2\frac{1}{4}$"

RUNNER MAKE TWO

$14\frac{1}{2}$"

Fig. 24-5. Plan for runners and for sides.

Fig. 24-6. Small sled.

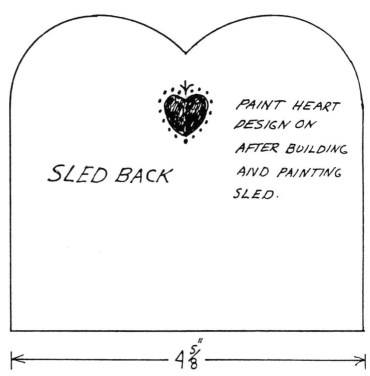

SLED BACK

PAINT HEART
DESIGN ON
AFTER BUILDING
AND PAINTING
SLED.

$4\frac{5}{8}''$

Fig. 24-7. Plan for seat back for large sled. Heart is painted on.

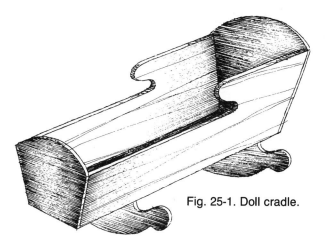

Fig. 25-1. Doll cradle.

Cradle

I took the pattern for this cradle from a very old cherry baby cradle that is in my family. It does not have a hood, but many of the early cradles had wooden hoods that shielded the baby's face and sometimes supported netting to keep flies away.

This little doll cradle is durable and will provide many hours of hard play. If you have a special doll, adjust the measurements to fit her perfectly. Generally, antique dolls are thin, and this pattern will fit most 10-13-inch dolls (Figs. 25-1, 25-2).

The cradle looks well stained or painted. I like to paint the doll's name or a Pennsylvania Dutch heart and flower motif on the headboard.

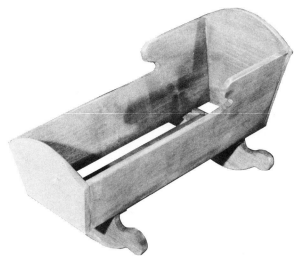

Fig. 25-2. Doll cradle before painting.

MATERIALS

Pine or Basswood:

- 1 piece, $1/4 \times 2^1/4 \times 11$ inches for rocker base
- 1 piece, $3/8 \times 2^3/4 \times 19$ inches for rockers
- 1 piece, $3/8 \times 5^1/8 \times 30$ inches for sides.
- 1 piece, $3/8 \times 6^1/2 \times 10^1/4$ inches for headboard and footboard.
- 1 piece, $3/4 \times 3^3/16 \times 8^1/2$ inches for braces
- 1 piece, $1/4 \times 4 \times 13^1/2$ inches for mattress base

- Carpenter's glue
- Small nails or brads
- Paint or stain, varnish

CONSTRUCTION TIPS

Cut two rocker pieces with the notches as shown in Fig. 25-5. Assemble (dry) to make sure they rock nicely. Sand, file, or wedge until they do. Glue and nail. Cut and sand cradle top pieces (Figs. 25-3, 25-4). Glue and nail together. Put rocker and cradle top together by gluing and nailing two braces on underside of rocker (Fig. 25-5). Paint or stain cradle. Cut a 4-$\times$-$13^1/2$-inch mattress base. Paint or stain, and pad. Glue, nail, or fit mattress base into cradle when everything is dry (Figs. 25-6, 25-7).

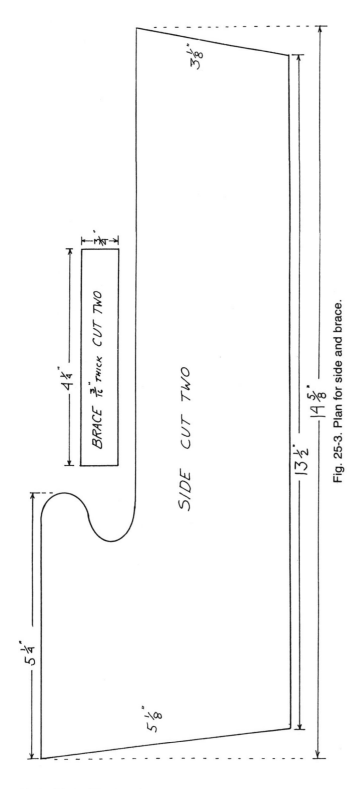

BRACE $\frac{3}{16}''$ THICK CUT TWO

$4\frac{1}{4}''$

$\frac{3}{4}''$

SIDE CUT TWO

$3\frac{1}{8}''$

$13\frac{1}{2}''$

$14\frac{5}{8}''$

$5\frac{1}{4}''$

$5\frac{1}{8}''$

Fig. 25-3. Plan for side and brace.

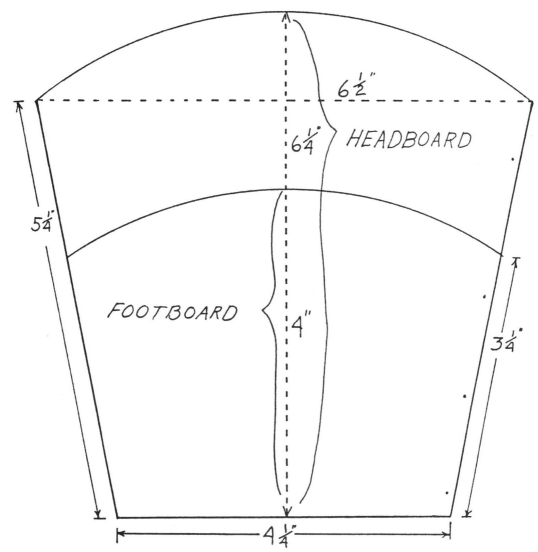

Fig. 25-4. Plan for footboard and headboard.

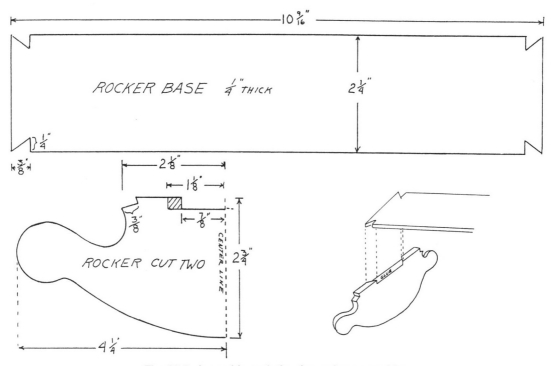

ROCKER BASE ¼" THICK

10⁹⁄₁₆"

2¼"

1¼"

⅜"

2⅛"

1⅛"

⅞"

⅜"

ROCKER CUT TWO

CENTER LINE

2¾"

4¼"

GLUE

Fig. 25-5. Assembly and plan for rocker assembly.

Fig. 25-6. Author putting rocker assembly together.

Fig. 25-7. Cradle.

Index

G

garrison house, miniature village, 123

H

hickory, x
household accessories, 3-42
   basket carrier, 18-22
   brackets for tab curtains, 10-12
   fruit dryer, 37-42
   knife tray, 13-17
   spoon rack, 4-9
   tray stand, 23-26
   wall box, 27-36

I

inn, miniature village, 120

K

knife tray, 13-17

L

lamb pull toy, 96-100
limberjack toy, 101-105

M

maple, x
miniature village, 117-125
   barn, 122
   basic house for, 117
   Cape Cod cottage, 123
   church for, 119
   covered bridge, 122
   eyebrow, one-and-a-half-story house, 124
   farmhouse and outbuilding, 121
   garrison house, 123
   inn and shop, 120
   saltbox house, 124
   shop building, 125
   Williamsburg cottage, 125

N

Noah's Ark, 106-116

O

one-and-a-half-story (eyebrow) house, miniature village, 124

P

painting, xiv
patterns
   enlarging, viii-ix
   transfering to wood, ix
peg rack, shelf and, 46-50
pine, x
plant stand, Victorian-style, 69-73
plate rack, dust-free, 60-68
poplar wood, x
power tools, viii, xiii
pull toy, lamb, 96-100

R

racks
   pegged, shelf and, 46-50
   plate, dust-free, 60-68

S

safety precautions, xiii-xiv
salt box, wall-mounted, 27-36
saltbox house, miniature village, 124
sanding, xiv
seating
   country bench, 55-59
   five-board stool, small, 51-54
settle table, 74-80
shop building, miniature village, 120, 125
sled, doll-sized, 152-157
small five-board stool, 51-54
spoon rack, 4-9
stains, xv
stands
   plant stand, Victorian, 69-73
   tray stand, folding, 23-26
stenciling, 133-134
step-by-step procedures, xv

T

table, settle and, hinged-top, 74-80
tools, viii, xii-xiii
toys (*see also* doll furniture), 91-140
   animals for Noah's ark, 108-116
   ferris wheel, 135-140
   lamb pull toy, 96-100
   limberjack, 101-105
   miniature village, 117-125
   Noah's Ark, 106-116
   woodchoppers, 92-95